"While many scholars have written about race and immigration, this book uniquely brings contemporary structures of racism and immigration to a wide variety of readers. Amid the political rhetoric of a 'post-racial society' the authors remind us that racism continues to exert deleterious effects on a variety of groups including immigrants. Equally importantly, this book reminds us about the racialization of two groups that remain less visible in the migration literature: highly skilled migrants and black immigrants. A very timely and useful book for scholars, practitioners, and a general audience of interested readers."

Bandana Purkayastha, University of Connecticut

"*Race and Immigration*'s serious examination of the relationship between immigration, race, and ethnicity is a welcome respite from the din of the acrimonious public debate on the costs and benefits of contemporary immigration. Chock-full of useful and up-to-date information on hotly contested immigration issues, it is a valuable resource for all those interested in social change."

Yến Lê Espiritu, University of California, San Diego

D0924390

Race and Immigration

Immigration & Society series

Thomas Faist, Margit Fauser & Eveline Reisenauer, *Transnational Migration*

Christian Joppke, *Citizenship and Immigration*

Grace Kao & Elizabeth Vaquera, *Education and Immigration*

Nazli Kibria, Cara Bowman & Megan O'Leary, *Race and Immigration*

Ronald L. Mize & Grace Peña Delgado, *Latino Immigrants in the United States*

Philip Q. Yang, *Asian Immigration to the United States*

Race and Immigration

*Nazli Kibria, Cara Bowman
and Megan O'Leary*

polity

Copyright © Nazli Kibria, Cara Bowman and Megan O'Leary 2014

The right of Nazli Kibria, Cara Bowman and Megan O'Leary to be identified as Author of this Work has been asserted in accordance with the UK Copyright, Designs and Patents Act 1988.

First published in 2014 by Polity Press

Polity Press
65 Bridge Street
Cambridge CB2 1UR, UK

Polity Press
350 Main Street
Malden, MA 02148, USA

All rights reserved. Except for the quotation of short passages for the purpose of criticism and review, no part of this publication may be reproduced, stored in a retrieval system, or transmitted, in any form or by any means, electronic, mechanical, photocopying, recording or otherwise, without the prior permission of the publisher.

ISBN-13: 978-0-7456-4791-3
ISBN-13: 978-0-7456-4792-0(pb)

A catalogue record for this book is available from the British Library.

Typeset in 11 on 13 pt Sabon by
Servis Filmsetting Ltd, Stockport, Cheshire
Printed and bound by Berforts Information Press Ltd.

The publisher has used its best endeavours to ensure that the URLs for external websites referred to in this book are correct and active at the time of going to press. However, the publisher has no responsibility for the websites and can make no guarantee that a site will remain live or that the content is or will remain appropriate.

Every effort has been made to trace all copyright holders, but if any have been inadvertently overlooked the publisher will be pleased to include any necessary credits in any subsequent reprint or edition.

For further information on Polity, visit our website: www.politybooks.com

Contents

Acknowledgments

Many thanks to the editors at Polity Press for their encouragement and support of this project. As is often the case with books, the writing of this one has stretched out for more years than anyone anticipated. We especially thank Jonathan Skerrett for his patience in sticking with us during the long duration of the project. We also gratefully acknowledge the support that we have received for the project from the Albert Morris Research Fund of the Department of Sociology at Boston University.

For all three of us, the opportunity to work together on this project has been a fruitful and enjoyable experience, even when it has been challenging. Whenever our energies have sagged, we have reminded each other of the importance of race and immigration as a topic of inquiry.

For Nazli Kibria, the students in her annual Sociology of International Migration seminars have been an important source of inspiration, constantly pushing her to think about immigration in different ways. Nazli is grateful to her family, especially to James Allen Littlefield, for his patience during the writing of the book. Nazli would like to dedicate this book to her daughter Shumita Kibria Littlefield, herself an aspiring author, for the love and joy that Shumita brings to her life.

Cara Bowman would like to thank her entire family for their love and encouragement throughout this process. She is grateful to her parents, Sheila and John Bowman, who are always enthusiastic and caring, and who taught her to question racial boundaries

Acknowledgments

from an early age. She dedicates this book to her partner, Juan Lopez, whose own experience challenging the racial order in the U.S. has brought deep personal significance to this work.

Megan O'Leary would like to thank her parents, Dan and Cindy O'Leary, for the endless support and love they bring into her life every day. She is grateful for the laughs and constant voice of reason provided by her sister, Erin O'Leary. She would also like to thank her extended family for cheering her on throughout her graduate career as vigorously as they do for the New England Patriots.

Both Cara and Megan would also like to thank Nazli for giving them the opportunity to produce such an important book, and for helping them to grow as scholars and writers throughout the process.

The authors hope this book will be a step not only towards understanding the challenges facing immigrants in the U.S. racial order, but that it also inspires movements to remedy such inequalities.

1

The Race–Immigration Nexus

I'm here today because the time has come for common-sense, comprehensive immigration reform. The time is now. Now is the time. Now
is the time. Now is the time.

I'm here because most Americans agree that it's time to fix a system
that's been broken for way too long. I'm here because business leaders,
faith leaders, labor leaders, law enforcement, and leaders from both
parties are coming together to say now is the time to find a better way
to welcome the striving, hopeful immigrants who still see America
as the land of opportunity. Now is the time to do this so we can
strengthen our economy and strengthen our country's future. Think
about it—we define ourselves as a nation of immigrants. That's who
we are—in our bones. The promise we see in those who come here
from every corner of the globe, that's always been one of our greatest
strengths. It keeps our workforce young. It keeps our country on the
cutting edge. And it's helped build the greatest economic engine the
world has ever known.

President Barack Obama, January 29, 2013

Around much of the world today, issues of global migration—of
movement across national borders—loom large in the political
arena. This is certainly the case in the United States, where in
the run-up to the 2012 Presidential election, immigration was
among the hot-button issues that occupied campaign rhetoric.
After winning a second term in office, President Obama spoke
fervently of the need to fix the country's "broken" immigration
system. As we see in the above excerpt from a Presidential speech

on immigration,[1] U.S. political discourse on immigration has often been couched in nationalist imagery, of America as the "land of opportunity" and a "nation of immigrants." Drawing on this imagery, in the early months of 2013 President Obama set out a specific plan for immigration reform that included employer accountability, pathways to legalization for immigrants without papers, as well as easier access to visas for high-skilled immigrants.

In the immigration debates of the U.S. today, the theme of race is perhaps most noticeable for its seeming invisibility. When it is mentioned, the distinctiveness of race is depicted as a matter that can be overcome with the passage of time and hard work; over time there is assimilation into the American melting pot. Of course this is far from being always the case. The passage of watershed laws in U.S. immigration history, such as the 1882 Chinese Exclusion Act and the 1924 National Origins Act, were marked by openly expressed and virulent racism. But in early twenty-first century America, an open agenda of racial exclusion is no longer legitimate. Instead, a variety of "race-blind" arguments mark the immigration debates. Thus those who contend that the U.S. needs to build a taller and tighter fence to guard the U.S.-Mexico border do not speak of race, but rather of the need to deter the criminal activities that surround the border regions. Those who argue against an amnesty program for undocumented immigrants do not speak of race, but instead dwell on the importance of rewarding those who follow the laws of the land and punishing those who do not abide by them. And those who assert the need to extend more opportunities for the highly skilled to come to the U.S. do not speak of race, but cite the need for the U.S. to remain competitive in the global economy.

As suggested by these examples, contemporary immigration debates in the U.S. have been framed by an assumption of "color-blindness" or the notion that "race" *should not* and in fact *does not* matter today, although it might have in the past. But we would argue that denial of the realities of race and their importance to immigration dynamics and processes in the U.S. does not reduce their significance. It only serves to obscure them. As Omi and Winant (1994) have put it: "Opposing racism requires that we notice race . . . that we afford it the recognition it deserves and the subtlety it embodies" (159).

A Race Optic and the Race–Immigration Nexus

We approach the study of immigration and race with a "race optic." To explain this further, let us first take a step back and define "race." In a race-conscious society such as the U.S., the answer to the question of what race is may seem obvious at first glance. In popular U.S. understandings, racial categories such as "black" and "white" are indicated by physical markers, most notably skin color, that in turn signal innate differences between people. But as we look at how the perceptions and meanings of the markers diverge across time and place, it becomes increasingly clear that these seemingly intrinsic differences are actually social and political constructions.

Drawing on critical race theories (Goldberg 1993; West 1995; Romero 2008), we see race as a political project rooted in histories of western colonialism and imperialism and thus marked by a core commitment to white privilege and power. We also understand race as "an organizing principle of society that persists on its own through its deep entrenchment in social structure and institutions, such that actors need not be conscious of their part in it to enjoy privilege allowing it to endure" (Weiner 2012: 333). Concurrently, race is an ongoing and constantly developing feature of power relations in society.

Specifically, we define a "race optic" to encompass the following ideas:

- Race is an ascribed difference, one that is given and used by those in power to define others as different and inferior from themselves in ways that maintain their own (the dominant group's) power.
- The ascribed differences of race are essentialized or widely understood to be based on "given," intrinsic group features.
- Physical distinctions, such as that of skin color, can be used

to draw boundaries between races and to signal intrinsic difference.

- Cultural differences, signaled by such markers as language, dress, and food, can be used to draw boundaries between races and to signal intrinsic difference.
- Racial formation or the social construction of race difference is organized by social institutions and the ideas and practices that are part of them.
- Racial boundaries have consequences for those who are defined by them, in terms of choices, opportunities, and resources.
- The dynamics of race interact with those of other axes of difference and inequality, including class, gender, nationality, and immigration status.

How does "race" compare with "ethnicity," a concept with which it is often paired? A popular definition is that racial boundaries emerge from physical differences between peoples in contrast to ethnic boundaries, which are a product of cultural differences. As Cornell and Hartmann (1998) have noted, this way of differentiating the concepts of race and ethnicity overlooks the central role of power and external assignment in the creation of racial boundaries. Race and ethnicity are both social constructions. But racial boundaries are especially rooted in the efforts of dominant groups to create distinctions that affirm their power and superiority. Rather than external assignment, the emergence of ethnic groups involves self-assertions of collective identity that are based on "perceived common ancestry, the perception of a shared history of some sort, and shared symbols of peoplehood" (1998: 32). But along with these differences in underlying dynamics, it is also the case that racial and ethnic boundaries can overlap, as those who find themselves defined by others as a group also come to see themselves in collective terms. Racial boundaries thus shape and constrain the terrain of ethnic identity, in some cases facilitating and in other cases restricting ethnic formations.

Our analysis of immigration draws on a "race optic" or a perspective that looks closely at the significance of race in relation to the social phenomena under study. A race optic on immigration urges us to consider a set of critical questions about the ways in which racial divisions both shape and are shaped by immigrant arenas and experiences. For example, how are changes in immigration law informed by contests of racial power and privilege? How are racial ideologies shaped by the strategies that immigrants use to get ahead in the labor market? Do these strategies affirm prevailing racial boundaries? Or do they challenge them, thus fomenting struggles and changes in the racial order?

By posing and addressing these and other questions, we analyze the "race–immigration nexus"—a fluid and intertwined bundle of linkages between race and immigration, specifically among the institutions, ideologies, and practices that define these arenas. In the chapters that follow we look at selected aspects of the U.S. immigrant experience—laws, occupations, and identity formations. Through in-depth analysis of selected episodes and cases in the United States, we explore how these various arenas have been part of the ongoing formation of the U.S. race–immigration nexus.

Throughout the world, in societies as diverse as Australia, France, Japan, and the United Arab Emirates, the politics of immigration, race, and nation are deeply intertwined. If there are important similarities in the race–immigration nexus of these societies, there are also vast differences, reflecting the particular conditions under which the nexus has emerged. In the case of the United States—the focus of this book—the national context has generated a race–immigration nexus that is marked by some notable themes. These include a national ideology of America as an immigrant country and a racial order in which a black-white division has played a pivotal role. We now turn to take a closer look at these themes and the many contradictions and uncertainties that have been part of them.

A Nation of Immigrants

Oscar Handlin (1951) has noted that the history of America is the history of the immigrant. Immigration has been central to the U.S. nation-building project. The colonization of North

America occurred through the establishment of settlements by European migrants in "the New World." The United States has also repeatedly sought labor from abroad in its quest for economic development. This import of labor has taken many different forms in the course of U.S. history, from the slave labor of Africans to the migrant labor of Europeans. In the contemporary United States, the labor market includes workers from abroad who toil in low-wage jobs in the agriculture and service industries, as well as high-skilled foreign professionals who are actively recruited by U.S. companies that are anxious to remain competitive in the global economy. Across these different circumstances, immigrants have been a vital part of the U.S. economy, past and present.

The importance of immigration to U.S. nation-building is also reflected in the country's ethos of national identity. Scholars often describe the United States as having an official doctrine of civic nationalism; it is adherence to shared civic values, such as commitment to freedom of religion, that binds the nation together. Civic nationalism signals the identity of America as an immigrant-receiving society. It suggests receptivity to the integration of immigrants, especially in contrast to ethnic nationalism, in which it is the idea of shared ancestry that gives meaning to national identity and community. More generally, immigration has been a key theme in the myths, symbols, and narratives of U.S. nationalism.

Underlying the idea of America as an immigrant country is a larger one—that of American exceptionalism. In this overarching narrative, the United States is an exceptional, even unique, country in human history and worldly affairs. It is a refuge of liberty, a moral leader that has been anointed by Divine Providence to assume a place of political and economic supremacy in the world. From the historical conquest of Native American lands to contemporary military campaigns abroad, American exceptionalism has provided "an unlimited charter for a kind of explicitly and sanctimoniously 'anti-colonial' imperialism" (De Genova 2012: 252). It has, in short, shrouded the nation's exercise of power in a veil of moral imperative.

The narrative of American exceptionalism is deeply entwined with that of America as an immigrant country. It is a country that in its special greatness, its commitment to freedom and opportunity, attracts people from all over the world. Consider, for example, the Statue of Liberty, that icon of American freedom, and the verse by Emma Lazarus that is inscribed beneath it:

Give me your tired, your poor,
Your huddled masses, yearning to breathe free,
The wretched refuse of your teeming shore.
Send these, the homeless, tempest-tost to me,
I lift my lamp beside the golden door![2]

The Statue of Liberty represents the idea of America as an immigrant nation. As it symbolically beckons immigrants to its shores, it also affirms the idea of America as a land of opportunity—of the American Dream. It is a place where dreams can come true, where immigrants can achieve success through hard work and determination. As they do so they also become American, merging into the great "melting pot" of America. Indeed, the exceptionalism of America stems also from its capacity to assimilate, to effectively integrate newcomers into its midst. In 1782, the French-American writer J. Hector St. John de Crèvecœur published an influential volume of narrative essays entitled *Letters from an American Farmer* in which he wrote:

What then is the American, this new man? He is either an European, or the descendant of an European, hence that strange mixture of blood, which you will find in no other country . . . He is an American, who, leaving behind him all his ancient prejudices and manners, receives new ones from the new mode of life he has embraced, the new government he obeys, and the new rank he holds. He becomes an American by being received in the broad lap of our great Alma Mater. Here individuals of all nations are melted into a new race of men.[3]

Nested in American exceptionalism, the notion of America as an immigrant country can mask the significance of larger political and economic conditions in shaping migration flows and settlements. That is, if America as a land of freedom and opportunity has attracted immigrants, it is also the case that America has actively sought immigrants to meet its economic needs. Immigrant flows to the United States have also often resulted from disruptions to immigrant homelands caused by U.S. policy abroad. As the United States has sought to expand and consolidate its power and influence in the world, it has spurred migration flows to the United States.

The notion of America as an immigrant country has another, quite different side. If the immigrant story is extolled as national myth, it is also the case that U.S. attitudes toward immigrants have frequently been colored by fear, hostility, and restrictive policy. The narrative of American exceptionalism plays into this duality of attitudes. If it is a country that is welcoming of immigrants, it is also one that must, in order to preserve its exceptional character, be discerning in whom it admits into the country. Not everyone can fit into the exceptional fabric of America. As John Higham documents in *Strangers in the Land* (1955), immigrants have faced the ire of nativists who have feared "that some influence originating abroad threatened the very life of the nation from within" (6). Peter Schrag (2010) argues that at the core of nativism is the idea that there are some groups who are not fit to become Americans due to their inherent qualities. The specific focus of nativist ire has fluctuated, in terms of who is targeted and for what reason: religious traditions or deficient culture. But the underlying sentiment—that these foreigners represent a threat to the American way of life—has been constant. He writes: "In almost every generation, nativists portrayed new immigrants as not fit to become real Americans: they were too infected by Catholicism, monarchism, anarchism, Islam, criminal tendencies, defective genes, mongrel bloodlines, or some other alien virus to become free men and women in our democratic society" (Schrag 2010: 4).

American exceptionalism with its many faces is at the heart of the U.S. race–immigration nexus. That is, it is the nationalist narrative of America as a land of immigrants in simultaneous play with the powerful currents of nativism in the country which have shaped race and immigration and the linkages between them. For example, the ideology of America as a land of immigrants has at times served to obscure the racialization of immigrants. In public discourse it has allowed for a certain veiling of nativist sentiment and its significance for race relations. Furthermore, we would argue that the interplay of seemingly contradictory forces in the American stance toward immigration—of glorifying and reviling immigrants—has generated a good immigrant–bad immigrant dynamic. That is, the reconciliation of nativism with the ideology of America as an immigrant nation has occurred in part through the differential assessment of immigrant groups. The "good immigrant" is one who is fit to become American, whereas the "bad immigrant" is not only unfit but a threat to the social and political fabric of America.

The Black-White Racial Divide in America

The U.S. race–immigration nexus is also shaped by a racial order of white dominance in which a division between black and white has played a pivotal, albeit shifting and contested role. The construction of a social and political divide between black and white peoples was integral to the early U.S. nation-building project. Starting in the eighteenth century, European settlers in North America turned to the enslavement of black Africans to fulfill the needs of a growing economy. Slavery was legitimated by emerging racist ideology that drew from the work of so-called "race scientists" of the time. Indeed, by the early 1800s, racial distinctions were firmly established in U.S. life as science, social norms, and government court decisions designated blacks as subhuman and protected the rights of whites to own black slaves.

The American Civil War (1861–1865) was accompanied by intensified public debate over the position and rights of blacks. The era of Reconstruction that ensued saw important reforms, including the granting in 1867 of voting rights to blacks. But the progress was shortlived. By 1877, blacks were subjected to disenfranchisement; they experienced de facto segregation in the North and de jure segregation through Jim Crow laws in the Southern states. This was a time of intense racial backlash as,

9

fearing displacement, white cotton-plantation owners and workers "clung more desperately than ever to the automatic social status that inhered in their white skins" (Fredrickson 2002: 86–7). The *Plessy v. Ferguson* ruling of 1896, which stated that blacks and whites should live "separate but equal" lives, gave the legal stamp of approval to segregation between blacks and whites.

In the years after World War Two, racial discrimination continued to mark the U.S. landscape in powerful and visible ways. For example, black Americans were largely unable to take advantage of the suburban housing boom of the 1950s due to the routine denial of low-cost housing loans to them. But there were also growing challenges to the prevailing racial order. As the United States and Allied forces battled the Hitler regime with its claims of racial superiority, the ideology of scientific racism that had been so prominent in the early twentieth century was repudiated. In 1950, UNESCO issued a statement saying that "science gave no support to the notion that human groups differed in 'their innate capacity for intellectual and emotional development'" (Fredrickson 2002: 128). At this time as well, the United States found itself struggling to justify the racial inequalities of its own national landscape as it asserted itself as the world's superpower. The inequalities were inconvenient, detracting as they did from American moral claims to world leadership through universal commitment to freedom.

In 1954, the Supreme Court made a landmark decision in the case of *Brown v. Board of Education of Topeka*. In that case the court ruled invalid the separate but equal doctrine, thus bringing into question the entire Jim Crow system. Under the leadership of such prominent African American figures as W. E. B. Du Bois, Malcolm X, and Martin Luther King, Jr., the Civil Rights movement that emerged used massive political protest and legal challenge to launch a period of intensified struggle against U.S. racial inequalities. In the backdrop of the movement, racial minorities forged new collective identities and political strategies of empowerment. There were also notable legislative victories, including the 1964 Civil Rights Act that banned discrimination based on "race, color, religion or national origin" in employment practices and public accommodations. The 1965 Voting Rights Act protected voting rights and the Fair Housing Act of 1968 banned discrimination in the sales and rental of housing.

In brief, the twentieth century saw important changes in the U.S. racial order, including the weakening in certain respects of the black-white racial divide that had been its key organizing feature. Race continues to be a significant aspect of U.S. life, however. The racism of the past, consisting of overt expressions of beliefs about the innate inferiority of minority groups, has become far less acceptable. Instead, what has emerged in its wake is a new racism, a racism that takes covert forms and expressions. Analyzing the rise of conservative political movements in the 1980s, Omi and Winant (1986) write of the use of "code words" or phrases and symbols in political discourse that "refer indirectly to racial themes, but do not directly challenge popular democratic or egalitarian ideals" (1986: 120). They also note the emergence of a racism that is organized around a color-blind ideology—the idea that race is no longer relevant.

Writing of the development of color-blind racism, Howard Winant (2008) notes that the current global racial order is one in which racial differences have been reinterpreted "as matters of culture and nationality, rather than as fundamental human attributes somehow linked to phenotype" (200). Embedded in the project of neoliberalism that has defined the late twentieth century and early twenty-first century, color-blind racism suggests that social inequalities stem from the inability of some individuals to compete in the market economy. In explaining these individual deficiencies, cultural explanations are invoked. Thus, even as color-blind racism self-consciously eschews the idea of intrinsic differences between people based on skin color, it turns to the language of deep-seated, "given" cultural predispositions. Racial difference comes to be understood as innate cultural difference.

Eduardo Bonilla-Silva (2003) has identified several different frameworks of color-blind racism. The first, abstract liberalism, uses the language of equal opportunity and free choice to legitimate the status quo. The second, naturalization, is captured by the idea that racial inequality is "just the way things are"—an expression of natural human tendencies. The third one—that of cultural racism—explains racial inequality to be a result of cultural deficiencies. The fourth, minimization, is the argument that racial discrimination is rare and isolated. Thus those who identify racism are "whiners" who are making exaggerated claims and needlessly complaining.

We contend that racism and the black-white racial divide remain significant features of U.S. life, notwithstanding extremely crucial and ongoing changes in race relations. The black-white dichotomy continues to pervade commonsense American understandings; it remains an important conceptual anchor in everyday efforts to categorize and make sense of the identity of others. Moreover, the institutional boundaries between black and white Americans, as reflected in patterns of residential segregation and income and educational inequalities, continue to be sharp.[4]

In summary, the black-white racial divide, along with all of the complex contradictions and shifts that have been part of it, is an important feature of the U.S. race–immigration nexus. Thus, among the issues faced by immigrants to the United States, both in the past and today, a primary one is that of how to position oneself within a racial order that is broadly organized around a dichotomy of black and white. For many immigrants, the issue has been especially vexing, challenging their efforts to successfully negotiate the social and political landscape of the United States.

Immigrants to the United States: A Brief Overview

In 2010, the U.S. immigrant population totaled almost 40 million, constituting 13 percent of the total U.S. population of 309.3 million. California, New York, Texas, and Florida were the states with the largest numbers of foreign-born residents. Figure 1.0 provides an overview of the development of the U.S. immigrant population over time, from 1850 (when information on the nativity of the U.S. population was first collected), to 2011.

The data show that in 1850, the foreign-born made up 9.7 percent of the total U.S. population, which at that time was 2.2

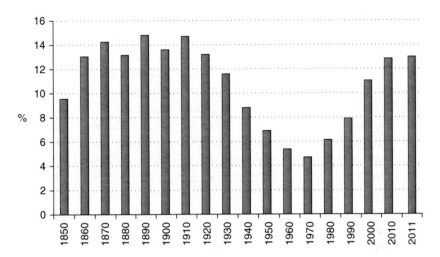

Figure 1.0   Foreign-Born as Percentage of the Total U.S. Population, 1850 to 2011

Note: The term "immigrants" refers to people residing in the United States who were not U.S. citizens at birth. This population includes naturalized citizens, lawful permanent residents (LPRs), certain legal nonimmigrants (e.g., persons on student or work visas), those admitted under refugee or asylee status, and persons illegally residing in the United States.

Source: The 2011 data are from the U.S. Census Bureau's American Community Surveys; the 2000 data are from Census 2000 (see www.census.gov). All other data are from Campbell Gibson and Emily Lennon, U.S. Census Bureau, Working Paper No. 29, Historical Census Statistics on the Foreign-Born Population of the United States: 1850 to 1990, U.S. Government Printing Office, Washington, D.C., 1999.

million people. The numbers rose rapidly in subsequent decades, with immigrants as a percentage of the total population peaking at 14.8 percent in 1890—a proportion that has not been exceeded since that time. But by 1930, following the passage of restrictive entry laws, the foreign-born at 14.2 million dropped to 11.6 percent of the U.S. population. The numbers continued to decline in subsequent decades, reaching a record low of 9.6 million foreign-born persons (4.7 percent of the U.S. population) in 1970. Since 1970, however, the tide has shifted, reflecting the passage

13

of liberalized immigration laws, specifically the Immigration and Nationality Act of 1965. The 1980s and 1990s saw a sharp rise in foreign-born numbers in the United States, mainly due to immigration from Latin America and Asia. In 1980, the foreign-born as a percentage of the total U.S. population stood at 6.2 (14.1 million persons). By 2000, the percentage had risen to 11.1 (31.1 million persons) and in 2011 to 13 (40 million persons). In short, the late twentieth and early twenty-first centuries have been an important time for immigration into the United States, similar in relative scope to the massive flows of the late nineteeth and early twentieth centuries.

Perhaps the most notable historical shift in U.S. immigration patterns lies in the origins of those entering the country. Until the late 1800s most immigrants were from Western Europe, including Britain, Ireland, Germany, Norway, and Sweden. By the early 1900s the pattern had changed as growing numbers of immigrants entered from such places as Italy, Austria-Hungary, and the Soviet Union. The 1970s saw yet another major shift, this time away from Europe and toward immigrants from Asia and Latin America. Figure 1.1 illustrates this historical shift in region of birth as a percentage of the total immigrant population from 1960 to 2010. We see that the percentage of the foreign-born population from Europe decreased from 74.5 percent of the total immigrant population in 1960 to 12.1 percent of the total immigrant population by 2010. The proportions of Latin American and Asian immigrants as percentages of the total immigrant population steadily increased over this period from 9.3 percent to 53.1 percent and 5 percent to 28.2 percent, respectively.

When we focus the data on specific source countries, we continue to see evidence of a dramatic historical shift. In 1960 and in 1970, Italy was the largest single source country, accounting for 13 percent and 10 percent, respectively, of the foreign-born population in the United States. However, since 1980, Mexico has occupied the top position. In 1980, 16 percent of the total foreign-born population was from Mexico, a number that rose to 21 percent in 1990 and to 29 percent in 2000.

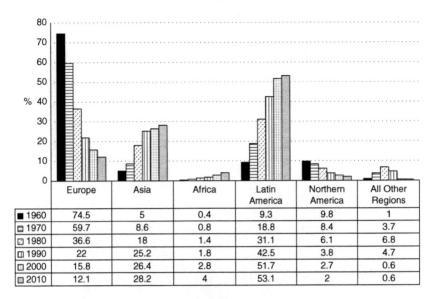

	Europe	Asia	Africa	Latin America	Northern America	All Other Regions
■ 1960	74.5	5	0.4	9.3	9.8	1
▤ 1970	59.7	8.6	0.8	18.8	8.4	3.7
▨ 1980	36.6	18	1.4	31.1	6.1	6.8
▥ 1990	22	25.2	1.8	42.5	3.8	4.7
▦ 2000	15.8	26.4	2.8	51.7	2.7	0.6
▢ 2010	12.1	28.2	4	53.1	2	0.6

Figure 1.1   Region of Birth as a Percentage of the Total Immigrant Population, 1960–2010

Source: Percentages manipulated from data available on the Migration Policy Institute Data Hub originally sourced from U.S. Census data, http://www.migrationinformation.org/datahub/charts/fb.2.shtml

Figure 1.2 offers information drawn from the U.S. Census Bureau's American Community Survey on top source countries for the foreign-born population in the United States in 2010. We see that at 29 percent of all foreign-born people residing in the United States, the Mexican-born were by far the largest immigrant group. Those from China occupied second place at 5 percent, closely followed by India and the Philippines (4 percent each). These four countries—together with Vietnam (3 percent), El Salvador (3 percent), Korea (3 percent), Cuba (3 percent), the Dominican Republic (2 percent), and Guatemala (2 percent)—made up 58 percent of all foreign-born persons residing in the United States in 2010. As we discuss further in Chapter Two, laws and policies on immigration have significantly affected the composition of the foreign-born population over time.

15

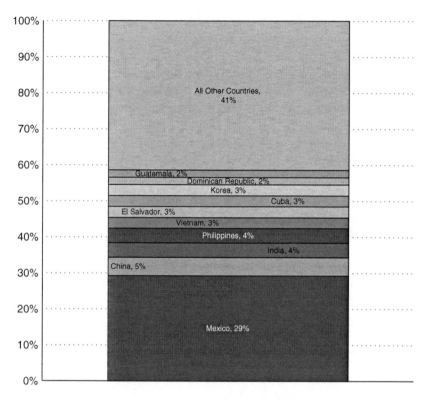

Figure 1.2 Ten Source Countries with the Largest Populations in the United States as Percentages of the Total Foreign-Born Population, 2010

Source: Data published on the Migration Policy Institute Data Hub, originally sourced from the U.S. Census Bureau, http://www.migrationinformation.org/ DataHub/charts/10.2010.shtml

Where do Immigrants in the United States Live?

As shown in Figure 1.3, immigrants are concentrated in certain areas of the country. In 2010, more than 1 in 4 foreign-born persons lived in California. Including California, New York, Texas, and Florida were home to more than half of all immigrants. This pattern of concentration has remained consistent since the early 1970s.

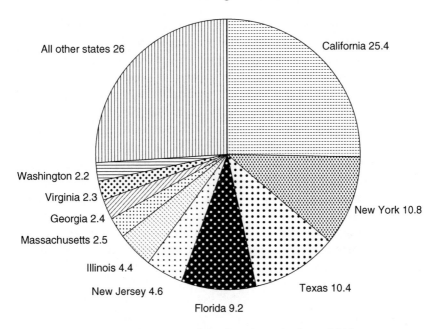

Figure 1.3   Foreign-Born Population by State, 2010

Note: Percentages do not sum to 100.0 due to rounding.

Source: U.S. Census Bureau, American Community Survey, 2010. Originally published in "The Foreign-Born Population in the United States: 2010." American Community Survey Reports, May 2012. http://www.census.gov/prod/2012pubs/acs-19.pdf

As we examine this historical pattern of concentration in certain states and gateway cities, we see the importance of family reunification and labor migration policies in immigrant settlement decisions. Prior to the contemporary wave of immigration, earlier waves of migrants typically settled in places that were close to their sending country (such as Mexican migration to Texas and the Southwest). They followed labor recruiters to work in cities or farms, or they settled in areas where there were opportunities to pursue entrepreneurial projects (Portes and Rumbaut 2006). As ethnic communities became established in certain locations, newer streams of migrants joined co-ethnic family and friends.

17

Immigration policy based on family reunification principles supported network-driven streams of migration, thus contributing to the concentration of immigrants in particular areas of the country. Moving to a region with a strong presence of co-ethnics often helps new migrants find social, cultural, and economic support, including the opportunity to enter into a particular ethnic niche in the labor market, as we discuss at length in Chapter Three.

When we look at locational decisions by immigrant groups through the race optic, however, we see that certain groups have faced greater constraints on these decisions due to their racial status. Most restricted have been black immigrant groups, including Afro-Caribbean and African immigrants. Examining census data from 1990 to 2000, scholars have found that despite small decreases in residential segregation from non-Hispanic whites for both foreign-born and native-born blacks in recent years, they continue to be more segregated from whites than other ethnic groups (Iceland and Scopilliti 2008). Unlike other ethnic groups that have chosen to settle in ethnic communities for social and economic support, black immigrant groups have experienced discriminatory practices that have channeled them into particular neighborhoods. Mary Waters notes that "racial segregation for blacks is unlike any other ethnic or immigrant group. It is far more extensive in scope, and it is not mitigated by class—segregation is just as severe for middle-class as for poor blacks" (1999: 243). Even when black immigrants try to move out of segregated neighborhoods that are rife with crime, poverty, and deteriorating schools, the new neighborhoods of choice tend to suffer from white flight and subsequently, disinvestment (Waters 1999).

In general, however, the late-twentieth century saw a decline in the extent of concentration in immigrant settlement. Immigrants are increasingly dispersed throughout the country (Lichter and Johnson 2006). In 2002, "no state received fewer than two hundred immigrants" (Portes and Rumbaut 2006: 47). These developments have contributed to the visibility of immigration as a national political issue in the United States, as communities across the country grapple with the presence of immigrants in their midst.

Among the conditions that have generated greater dispersal in immigrant settlement is the emergence in the late twentieth century of a government regime of immigration enforcement that has targeted particular groups of "visible minorities" such as Mexican immigrants. With stricter border-control measures, unauthorized migrants have crossed at more remote points and utilized professional smuggling networks in efforts to avoid armed border patrol officers (Portes and Rumbaut 2006). Immigrants have also moved east from traditional southwestern states to pursue newly emerging employment opportunities. Also of relevance is the growth of anti-immigrant sentiment in traditional gateway cities. In his discussion of how Los Angeles began to deflect Mexican immigrants, Light (2007) cites declining industrial employment compounded by political pressure resulting in political efforts to discourage immigrant settlement. As the city worked to actively sanction sweatshops and slums and to prevent low-income housing development in the suburbs, Mexican immigrants were encouraged to settle in other parts of the country.

The trend towards dispersal away from established gateway cities such as New York and Los Angeles has also been especially apparent among immigrants with high amounts of human capital. Immigrants who have migrated here as skilled professionals in fields such as medicine, science, and engineering tend to settle where they have received job offers. Many Indian immigrants, for example, have high levels of education and occupation skills. These resources mean that they tend to be less dependent on ethnic connections in the initial phase of settlement, resulting in dispersed clusters of Indian American settlement across the United States (Kibria 2006).

Where immigrants choose to settle in the United States clearly has important consequences for the organization of their lives, including the particular education and economic opportunities that are available to them. Regardless of where they live and work, immigrants must negotiate existing laws, social norms, and the local community's reception of their presence.

Immigrants' Educational and Occupational Attainment

As mentioned, contemporary migration to the United States is composed of immigrants representing a variety of racial and ethnic groups that were previously barred from migration due to racially restrictive National Origins quotas. The foreign-born population is also diverse in their levels of educational attainment and the variety of occupations they fill upon entering the United States. The Immigration and Nationality Act of 1965, structured around work and family reunification, contributed to this heterogeneity by recruiting both high-skilled and low-skilled workers who occupy jobs at the top and bottom, contributing to the hourglass economy. Specifically, the second half of the twentieth century brought the movement of many manufacturing jobs overseas, and increased the need for unskilled work in services to accommodate the growing FIRE (Finance, Insurance, Real Estate) sectors. Additionally, migrant flows that originally consisted primarily of highly skilled laborers later sent for family members with a more varied array of education levels and skill sets, further diversifying the composition of the foreign-born population (Portes and Rumbaut 2006).

Table 1.0 illustrates the overall percent distribution of the foreign-born and native-born age twenty-five or older in the U.S. labor force by educational attainment. The foreign-born were

Table 1.0:   Percent Distribution of the Foreign-Born and Native-Born, Age Twenty-five or Older, in the U.S. Labor Force by Educational Attainment, annual averages, 2011

Educational Attainment	Foreign-Born	Native-Born
Less than a high school diploma	25.5	5.3
High school graduates, no college	25.3	28.7
Some college or associate degree	17.5	29.9
Bachelor's degree and higher	31.7	36.1
Total	**100.0**	**100.0**

Source: Bureau of Labor Statistics, http://www.bls.gov/opub/ted/2012/ ted_20120606_data.htm

more likely than the native-born to have less than a high school diploma as their highest level of educational attainment at age twenty-five or older. Just over 25 percent of the foreign-born in the labor force had high school as their highest level of education compared to 28.7 of the native-born in 2011. Consistent with the needs of the hourglass economy, however, 31.7 percent of foreign-born immigrants in the labor force possessed a bachelor's degree or higher, compared to 36.1 percent of the native-born population.

Interestingly, the levels of education of immigrants have stayed consistent since 1970.[5] The percentage of immigrants with a higher education degree and those with a high school degree or less is about the same. Because of the large increase in the immigrant population since the 1970s, however, there are now greater numbers of immigrants with lower education than there were previously. As we will see in our discussion of the labor market niches of immigrants, the levels of education also differ according to region. The Brookings Institution finds that "almost half of immigrants from Latin America arrive with less than a high school diploma, while about half of immigrants from Asia arrive with a bachelor's degree or higher."[6] This divergence in education levels is visible in the regional immigrant occupational patterns that we see emerging throughout the United States.

Where Do Immigrants in the United States Work?

According to data from the 2010 U.S. Census, the foreign-born were more likely to be employed in the U.S. labor force than the native-born population. Despite this high aggregate level of employment, the data on occupations and specific industries reveal the importance of the intersectionality of gender, race, and immigration status in determining employment opportunities available to new immigrants.

As seen in Table 1.1, 21.8 percent of foreign-born men worked in natural resources, construction, and maintenance in 2011 compared to only 15.7 percent of native-born men. Similarly, employed foreign-born men are more likely than native-born men to work in service occupations and production, transportation,

Table 1.1:   Percent of Foreign-Born and Native-Born Men and Women
Employed in Each Occupational Group, Annual Averages, 2011

	MEN		WOMEN	
	Foreign-born	Native-born	Foreign-born	Native-born
Management, business, and financial operations	11.2	17.7	10.7	14.8
Professional and related	15.4	18.4	20.9	27.9
Service	19.3	13.7	32.2	19.4
Sales and office	12.6	17.6	24.5	32.6
Natural resources, construction, and maintenance	21.8	15.7	1.5	0.7
Production, transportation and material moving	19.8	16.9	10.1	4.7
Total Employed	**100.0**	**100.0**	**100.0**	**100.0**

Source: Bureau of Labor Statistics, U.S. Department of Labor, *The Editor's Desk*, Education and occupations of the foreign born in 2011 on the Internet at http://www.bls.gov/opub/ted/2012/ted_20120606.htm (visited November 29, 2012)[7]

and material-moving occupations. In contrast, native-born men are more likely than foreign-born men to work in professional and related occupations and sales and office jobs. Employed foreign-born women were more likely to be in service occupations at 33.2 percent compared to only 19.4 percent of employed native-born women.

Table 1.2, based on data from the American Community Survey, offers information on immigrant involvement in different sectors of the economy. We see that over 28 percent of civilian employed foreign-born persons aged sixteen or older work in management, business, science and arts occupations. These arenas are especially prominent among those from Northern America (59 percent), Asia (47 percent), Europe (45 percent), Oceania (41 percent) and Africa (38 percent). Service occupations are also prominent, engaging just over 25 percent of all foreign-born workers in comparison to

Table 1.2: Occupations of Immigrants by Country of Origin, 2010

	Manage-ment, Business, Science, & Arts	Service	Sales & Office	Natural Resources, Construc-tion, & Mainte-nance	Production, Transpor-tation, & Material Moving
Africa	37.7	24.8	19.8	3.3	14.4
Asia	47.4	17.5	21	3.4	10.6
Europe	44.6	16.7	19.4	8.5	10.7
Northern America	59	9.3	21.1	4.6	6
Oceania	40.9	19.5	22.6	6.8	10.3
Latin America	14.1	31.2	15.6	19.8	19.3
Mexico	8.6	31.3	12.6	25.2	22.3
Other Central America	10.9	34.6	14.5	20.5	19.5
South America	27.5	27.5	21.7	10.6	12.7
Caribbean	24.8	30.4	21.7	8.4	14.7
Native	37.4	16.6	26.4	8.4	11.2
Foreign Born	28.6	25.1	17.8	13	15.5
Total	**35.9**	**18**	**25**	**9.1**	**11.9**

Source: U.S. Census Bureau, American Community Survey, 2010. Originally published in "The Foreign-Born Population in the United States: 2010." American Community Survey Reports, May 2012: http://www.census.gov/prod/2012pubs/acs-19.pdf

16.6 percent of native-born workers. Among immigrant workers from Latin America, 31 percent are in service occupations and 40 percent are in the fields of natural resources, construction, maintenance, production, transportation and material moving.

The general picture that is offered by the above data is of diversity coupled with polarization. That is, immigrants are present in varied sectors of the U.S. labor market, with notable clusters at both the upper and lower ends. They are found then in both "good" and "bad" jobs that differ widely in terms of such qualities as pay, prestige, working conditions and opportunities for mobility. Reflecting this bimodal pattern, immigrants today constitute an important segment of professional workers in the life sciences and information technology fields. At the same time, immigrant workers are prominent in such industries as accommodation, agriculture, and construction, especially in the low-end jobs within them. For example, within the accommodation industry, immigrant workers are more likely to work as maids and housekeepers than the native-born, who dominate managerial and desk clerk positions. Similarly, in agriculture, most immigrants are low-skilled farmworkers, while more than one-third of U.S.-born workers in this industry occupy the more privileged positions of farmers and ranchers. And in the construction industry, U.S.-born workers hold more managerial positions than the foreign-born, who are more likely to be laborers (Brookings Institute 2012). Broad divisions of origin among immigrants also mark the bimodal labor market pattern. Reflecting their higher levels of education, foreign-born workers from Asia and Europe are far more likely than those from Latin America to work in management, business, and science arenas where "good jobs" are more common.

When we examine the trajectories of college-educated immigrants in the workforce, the race–immigration nexus becomes even more prominent. In 2008, the Migration Policy Institute used data from the New Immigrant Survey and the American Community Survey to discuss the issue of "brain waste" or "skill underutilization" affecting one out of every five high-skilled immigrants in the United States (Batalova, Fix, and Creticos 2008). In addition to factors such as demonstrating English language proficiency, having a U.S. college degree versus a foreign degree, and entering under an employment visa, the researchers found that region of birth disproportionately affected employment and skill utilization for the foreign-born (Batalova et al. 2008).

Despite high levels of academic achievement, Latin American and African-born highly skilled immigrants confronted more challenges in the labor market. These groups consistently faced unemployment and skill underutilization more than immigrants from European and Asian countries. We suspect that racial discrimination, entrenched ideas of colonialism and empire, ethnic niches, and contexts of reception affect occupational attain-

Table 1.3: Percent Naturalized by Period of Entry, 2010

	Before 1980	1980–1989	1990–1999	2000 or later
Africa	87.5	77.5	64.3	21.5
Asia	91.8	85.5	67.9	18.8
Europe	83.4	67.1	63.2	22.3
Northern America	70.7	49.3	34.5	9.5
Oceania	65.1	58.1	43.9	11.4
Latin America	72.3	49.7	25.1	8.9
Mexico	*61.8*	*36.0*	*14.5*	*5.1*
Other Central America	*76.7*	*52.0*	*23.2*	*7.8*
South America	*85.8*	*74.1*	*46.3*	*14.2*
Caribbean	*86.0*	*70.4*	*52.0*	*18.5*
Foreign Born	**79.8**	**63.1**	**42.9**	**13.7**

Source: "The Foreign-Born Population in the United States: 2010." American Community Survey Reports. ACS-19. Washington, D.C.: U.S. Census Bureau. http://www.census.gov/prod/2012pubs/acs-19.pdf

ment for immigrants beyond educational attainment and chain migration. As we discuss in Chapter Three, a process we call "occupational racialization" contributes to the channeling of racial groups into certain professions, affecting the identities and life chances for particular ethnic groups, and for generations to follow.

Another critical influence in the educational opportunities and occupational paths that immigrants take is their citizenship status. As shown in Table 1.3 above, those immigrants who have lived in the United States for longer periods of time are more likely to be naturalized citizens, which also opens up a much wider array of jobs. Interestingly, Mexico has the lowest percentage of naturalized citizens in any given decade. As we highlight in Chapter Two, the conflicting U.S. policies surrounding the recruitment and then restriction of Mexican workers has impeded a clear legal path to citizenship for the millions of Mexicans residing in the United States.

Our goal in this book is to offer insights into the dynamics of interaction between race and immigration in the United States. In the chapters that follow we explore selected features of immigrant life. Chapter Two ("Immigration Policy and Racial Formations") looks at the history of U.S. immigration law, from the Chinese Exclusion Act of 1882 to the 2010 passage by the state of Arizona of SB 1070 (Senate Bill 1070), aimed at discouraging irregular immigrants from entering or remaining in the state. In Chapter Three ("Race and the Occupational Strategies of Immigrants"), we explore the role of immigrant workers in the contemporary U.S. labor market. We offer a number of intensive case studies of jobs and occupations in which immigrant labor has been especially prominent. Chapter Four ("Immigrant Identities and Racial Hierarchies") turns to the development of immigrant identities. Our focus here is on the various strategies by which immigrant groups have tried to navigate the racial order, while achieving a sense of belonging, affiliation, and community in the United States.

Throughout our explorations of immigrant life, we focus on the question of how racial structures and ideologies have entered into the development of these arenas and also, in turn, been shaped by them. Each of these spheres—laws, occupations, and identities—offers a sharp window into the interactive dynamics of race and immigration.

2

Immigration Policy and Racial Formations

"Immigration policy" refers to the laws, institutions, practices, and approaches that nations establish to govern the movement and settlement of noncitizens into their borders. These shifting and often contested national regulations are at the heart of the immigrant experience, shaping immigrant lives and communities in myriad and powerful ways.

In this chapter we explore the development of U.S. immigration policies. Using a race optic, we look at the multifaceted and interactive relationship between immigration policy and racial conditions. The development of immigration policy has not only reflected racial dynamics, but it has also played a crucial formative role in the U.S. racial order. We focus on three broad eras in the history of U.S. immigration policy. The era of restriction, from the late nineteenth through the early twentieth century, was a time of emerging immigration controls for the United States. The developing immigration regime helped to deepen the significance of race in the U.S. nation-building project. In the late 1940s, activists rose up in response to racial violence and discrimination, culminating in the Civil Rights movement of the 1950s and 1960s. The changes wrought by the Civil Rights movement influenced the next major immigration reforms, defined by the 1965 Immigration and Nationality Act. This Act reflected a movement away from the explicit racial exclusions of the previous era, and toward a more open and "race-neutral" approach. The quotas based on national origins were ostensibly eradicated, greatly increasing the racial

27

and ethnic diversity of the immigrants who subsequently entered the United States.

However, the 1965 Act has been revised several times and while the increased flow of diverse immigrants has challenged and reshaped the racial order of the country, racial inequality persists. Starting in the late twentieth century, a restrictive course of immigration policy has been apparent. The contemporary era of enforcement has been one in which the stricter policing of borders has been a particular focus of immigration policy. Again, though not openly racist, these laws, by effectively vilifying large categories of immigrants, have served as an important anchor of racial dynamics. More generally, as we will see, what these three eras of immigration enforcement have in common is a constant tension between the need for, and active recruitment of, immigrant labor to the U.S. economy alongside demands for restriction that are buoyed by ongoing currents of nativist sentiment.

Race and Nation-Building: The Era of Restriction

The mid-nineteenth to early twentieth century was a time of massive immigration. In 1890, the foreign-born as a percentage of the total U.S. population reached a historic peak of almost 15 percent, a figure that has not been exceeded since that time. The "pull" forces behind this influx included a rapidly industrializing U.S. economy and an accompanying demand for labor. Not only did the number of immigrants rise during this period, but there was also greater diversity in the origins of those coming into the country. While in the early 1800s it was Northern and Western Europe, by the end of the century it was the Southern and Eastern parts of Europe that dominated as sending regions.

There were also flows from other parts of the world. In the mid-1800s thousands of Chinese, largely young men from the southern regions of China, came to work in the expanding western frontiers of the United States. Many toiled on the massive project of building the transcontinental railway. While relatively few in number, certainly in comparison to the other movements of the time, the

Chinese soon found themselves to be the target of immense hostility. White settlers identified the Chinese as competitors who were unfairly taking over available jobs because of a willingness to accept lower wages. What ensued was an organized political campaign of exclusion that sought to end Chinese migration and to restrict the rights of those Chinese already present in the United States. These efforts eventually culminated in the 1882 Chinese Exclusion Act, the first U.S. immigration law specifically designating a group as ineligible for entry on the basis of their ancestry. Besides barring Chinese people from entering the country, the Act also explicitly denied naturalization rights to the Chinese, categorizing them as "aliens ineligible for citizenship."

The movement to exclude the Chinese emphasized not only the theme of labor market competition, but also the larger threats posed by the Chinese to the moral core of America, a country driven by "manifest destiny"—a unique "mission" of democracy and progress.[1] Nativists accused the Chinese of being "dangerous," "deceitful and vicious," "criminal," "cowardly," and "inferior from the mental and moral point of view" (Schrieke 1936: 110). As evidenced by these inborn traits, they were racially inferior, making them unfit for membership and belonging in America. In her analysis of the anti-Chinese campaign, Erika Lee (2003) notes the parallels between the representation of African slaves and Chinese migrants, though the latter were seen as especially threatening due to their fundamental incapacity for assimilation:

> Both the "bought" Chinese prostitute and "enslaved" Chinese coolie were conflated with African American slaves. Racial qualities commonly assigned to African Americans were used to describe Chinese immigrants. Both were believed to be heathen, inherently inferior, savage, depraved, and lustful. Chinese, like African Americans, were "incapable of attaining the state of civilization of the Caucasian." And while some believed the Chinese were "physiologically and mentally" superior to African Americans, they were more of a threat, because they were less assimilable (Lee 2003: 27).

The 1882 laws had a devastating impact on the growth of the Chinese American community. In the aftermath of the Act, many

29

Chinese returned home. Those who remained found themselves segregated and confined to a limited range of difficult jobs. While most were unable to bring over kin from China, some did so through their U.S. citizenship, which gave them the ability to sponsor family members. Such sponsorship efforts were facilitated by the infamous 1906 San Francisco earthquake and fire, which destroyed much of the city and its municipal records, including those of Chinese immigration and citizenship. Under these circumstances, U.S. authorities could not readily contest claims of U.S. citizenship by the Chinese residents of California (Daniels 2004: 24).

The Chinese Exclusion Act is widely seen as a landmark, a defining moment in the history of U.S. immigration laws. With it, the United States formally became a "gatekeeping" nation and immigration laws came to hold a self-conscious place in the American nation-building project. Indeed, the 1882 Chinese Exclusion Act marks the era of expansion for restrictive U.S. immigration laws. In 1917, a series of exclusionary laws were enacted. At a time when literacy was not the norm in many parts of the world, immigrants became subject to a literacy test. An "Asiatic Barred Zone" was established with the goal of ensuring that immigration from Asia, including South Asia and Southeast Asia, did not occur.[2] Several classes of persons were excluded from entry, including anarchists, those with physical or mental defects, children unaccompanied by parents, and women coming for "immoral purposes." And in an extremely important provision, the 1917 laws also mandated the deportation of those in the United States who were found to be "public charges" or to meet, post-facto, the various criteria for denial of entry.

The era of immigration restriction reached a pinnacle in 1924, when Congress passed the Johnson-Reed Act. Also known as the National Origins Act, these laws essentially sought to barricade the United States against the entry of immigrants from around the world, with the exception of northern and western Europe. The successful passage of the National Origins Act marked a great triumph for the forces of racist nativism. Fortified by the "science" of race eugenics, those in favor of the Act expressed alarm about the influx of persons of inferior racial stock. These persons, they argued, were decidedly unsuited to be Americans and were in fact a danger to the Anglo-Saxon, Nordic character of the country. The specific provisions of the laws included a national limit on the annual numbers of immigrants coming into the United States; with the exception of those from the Americas, (including Canada and Mexico), immigration from different countries of the world also became subject to specified quotas of visas according to national origins. The quotas were calculated using a formula that measured the supposed ratio of different nationalities among inhabitants of the United States in 1890 (later changed to 1920) with the goal of limiting immigration to according proportions.[3] Several classes of persons were not acknowledged as inhabitants of the United States and thus excluded altogether from the calculations. They included: "(1) immigrants from the [Western Hemisphere] or their descendants, (2) aliens ineligible for citizenship or their descendants, (3) the descendants of slave immigrants, or (4) the descendants of the American aborigines."[4]

The Consolidation of Whiteness

From the Chinese Exclusion Act of 1882 to the National Origins Act of 1924, the immigration regime of the late nineteenth and early twentieth century helped to articulate and establish racial exclusion as a core principle of immigration policy, and more broadly, of the U.S. nation-building project. Indeed, these laws upheld ideologies of America as a "white nation" at a time of important flux in the U.S. racial order. David Goldberg argues that the latter part of the nineteenth century was an especially critical time for the project of U.S. nationalism and white privilege due to important challenges to the racial order. The collapse of slavery within the country coupled with the growth of visible anticolonial struggles around the world threatened the coherence of white identity, generating insecurity about its attendant privileges. He writes of how, under these conditions, "Whiteness . . . needed to be renegotiated, reaffirmed, projected anew. . . . From this point on . . . whiteness explicitly and self-consciously became a state project" (2001: 181).

With a sense of urgency related to these conditions, the immigration regime of the late nineteenth and early twentieth century affirmed racial exclusion and white privilege. As we have seen, the immigration laws of 1882, 1917, and 1924 proffered a racialized understanding of American national identity. This was an understanding in which some groups were inherently unsuited to join the American nation, a community essentially defined by its whiteness. Analysts of the National Origins Act of 1924 and its associated campaigns have noted the important role that it played in diffusing the concepts and vocabulary of race into the popular American consciousness. As it institutionalized the restriction of immigrants on the basis of nationality, the Act articulated and legitimated race classification as a system for assessing human beings and their value (Carter, Green, and Halpern 1996).

Embedded as it was in the racial order of the United States, however, the immigration regime of the late nineteenth and early twentieth century also raised incipient points of uncertainty and tension within this order and the project of whiteness. This included the question of how to define the *racial* boundaries of white identity. Whereas groups such as the Chinese seemed to present relatively little ambiguity with respect to their nonwhite status, the situation of Europeans who were not of Anglo-Saxon or Nordic descent was less clear-cut. As we have mentioned, among the specific issues animating the 1924 Act was alarm over high levels of settlement from southern and eastern Europe. For example, Italians, Jews, and Poles were portrayed by nativists as innately unsuited to be Americans. Indeed, these newcomers were widely seen as racially inferior, as Nancy Foner (2005) describes in her writings on the history of immigration to New York:

[Southern and eastern Europeans] . . . were seen as racially different from—and inferior to—people with origins in northern and western Europe. They were believed to have distinct biological features, mental abilities and innate character traits. They looked different to most New Yorkers and were thought to have physical features that set them apart—facial features often noted, for example, in the case of Jews, and "swarthy" skin, in the case of Italians. (13)

But if the National Origins Act of 1924 affirmed the racial marginality of southern and eastern Europe, there were other legal contexts in which these groups were designated as "white." Most important, perhaps, southern and eastern Europeans were recognized in legal and political terms as "white," a fact that gave them access to U.S. citizenship and its accompanying privileges, such as the right to vote and to own land. Historians have noted that in late nineteenth and early twentieth century America, this notion of "inferior whites," with the simultaneity of racial stigma and whiteness that it implies, did not seem as contradictory as it tends to appear to American sensibilities today. The correspondence of race and color that is so much a part of commonsense understandings of race in the contemporary United States had not yet fully developed at this time.

While the questions surrounding the concept of whiteness remained, as time passed a more unitary notion of whiteness had gained currency in the United States by the mid-twentieth century. The coupling of racial stigmatization with a legal designation as "white" continued to shadow the experiences of many, particularly Mexicans who were not white, but they were not black either. Nonetheless, the idea of race and color as largely overlapping matters developed. Underlying this consolidation of whiteness were the improved social and economic circumstances of those of southern and eastern European descent in the United States. With their success, their previously highlighted racial differences from Anglo-Saxon and Nordic peoples declined in significance. Indeed, by the 1960s the descendants of the Italian, Jewish, and Polish immigrants who had been so virulently opposed at an earlier time had made considerable strides toward acceptance by the dominant, white U.S. society. The sharp decline in immigration flows that followed the 1924 Act may have contributed to this acceptance by quieting anti-immigrant sentiment and reducing the hostility faced by the settlers. Also, many were able to take advantage of the expanding manufacturing sector to obtain factory work. These jobs provided relatively secure employment as well as an effective gateway into the middle-class rungs of the U.S. economy. From this location, the descendants of these European immigrants were well positioned to take advantage of the opportunities generated by the U.S. economic boom of the post–World War Two years, a time when the ranks of the middle class expanded.

The successful integration of late nineteenth and early twentieth-century European immigrants served to consolidate and strengthen the boundaries of "whiteness." As those of southern and eastern European descent came to be seen as white in an unqualified sense, the dangers of a "fractured whiteness" that had seemed so imminent in earlier decades, gradually dissipated. With this resolution of whiteness came an affirmation of black–white difference as the core feature—the central organizational axis—of the racial order. Indeed, scholars have written of how an effort to achieve distance from blacks was an important strategy of upward social mobility for European immigrants (Brodkin 2002; Ignatiev 1995; Roediger 1991[2007]). In other words, in the struggle for acceptance from U.S. society, they emphasized collective difference and separation from blacks.

The trajectory of European integration into the United States reinforced a racial order organized around a dichotomy of black and white, while simultaneously informing a powerful dynamic of division among immigrants. A history of the triumphant assimilation of once-stigmatized European immigrant groups is deeply embedded in popular American narratives of immigration. It is a history that is frequently invoked as positive proof of America as a country that welcomes immigrants and provides them with opportunities to achieve the American Dream. Concomitantly, it is a history that has also served as an enduring reference point for the construction of a good immigrant–bad immigrant dichotomy in U.S. culture. The successful assimilation of European immigrants is used to condemn "bad immigrants" who are deemed unassimilable, decisively locked out of full acceptance in America due to their own innate deficiencies.

Constructing "Illegal Immigration"

As the United States became a gate-keeping nation, it also created a particular category of immigrant, one that has played a key role in the construction of a good immigrant–bad immigrant dichotomy. This was the "illegal immigrant," the foreign national who was in the United States but without legal authorization. In the early twentieth century, unauthorized status was for the first time actively produced through the extension of such requirements as literacy and "no public charge" rules for immigrants to include post facto circumstances. That is, those who had already moved to the United States but did not meet these requirements could be deemed illegal and thus subject to deportation. The 1924 National Origins Act established a "consular control" system in which aliens were required to obtain a visa from a U.S. consulate office abroad before seeking entry. With this, immigrants who were in the United States without a visa became, in effect, irregular in their presence in the country. As DeSipio and de la Garza have described in their analysis of the 1924 National Origins Act:

> Without realizing it, Congress created a new category of immigrant through the establishment of categories of immigrants ineligible to immigrate—the undocumented immigrant. These were immigrants residing in the United States who had entered without advance approval, who had entered despite having the characteristics or traits specifically prohibited among immigrants (nationality, illness, criminal record, or beliefs), or, in later years, those who had entered the United States on a temporary basis and had remained beyond the authorized period. (1998: 40)

Over time, the emergence of illegal immigration as an institution was to have enormous consequences for the U.S. racial order. Since the early twentieth century, the label of "illegal" has been a potent vehicle of racialization for many immigrant groups, especially Mexicans. As mentioned earlier, the 1924 Act placed immigrants from the Americas outside the national quota system. Agribusiness had vigorously lobbied for this exception, citing the need to preserve access to Mexican labor, a longstanding feature of the economy of the Southwest. Even as this exemption seemed to confer advantages to Mexican immigrants, the institutions of illegality simultaneously created disadvantage. A long history of social and economic ties coupled with the extensive and often porous borders of Mexico and the United States meant that Mexican immigrants were especially vulnerable to charges of unauthorized presence. This became sharply apparent just a few years after the 1924 Act, with the onset of the Great Depression. Especially in California, Mexicans became a convenient scapegoat for economic and social problems. What followed were mass-scale deportations in which at least 500,000 and up to possibly one million Mexicans were forcibly repatriated on the grounds of their illegal presence in the United States (Mize and Delgado 2012: 21).

By the early 1940s, however, the United States actively recruited Mexican labor in response to the labor shortages of World War Two. From 1942 to 1964, a temporary worker scheme called the Bracero Program was instituted to recruit Mexican contract workers in agriculture and railroad building, primarily in the Southwest. In the midst of this program, in 1954, the U.S. government put forward a campaign called Operation Wetback, whereby Border Patrol officers used raids and roadblocks to find and deport irregular immigrants, primarily Mexicans. This pattern, of the active recruitment of labor from Mexico by U.S. industries accompanied by periodic campaigns of deportation, has been a recurring feature of Mexican movements to the United States. As we explore in greater detail later, it is a pattern that has informed the racialization of Mexican Americans and more generally of Latino/as, in critical ways.

The Immigration and Nationality Act of 1965: The Era of Reform

The years after World War Two saw growing demands for reform of the existing immigration regime. As Zolberg writes: "By the early 1960s many Americans regarded the national-origins system as on a par with deliberate segregation, contrary to the spirit of the Constitution, and few were prepared to defend it explicitly" (2001: 30). A variety of conditions made these immigration laws, along with the overt racism that guided them, less acceptable than in the past. This was a time when "scientific racism," so firmly lodged just a few decades earlier, faced repudiation. A flourishing Civil Rights movement was mounting crucial challenges to the racial order. And as a rising world superpower, the United States sought to distance itself from racism with an eye to gaining moral ascendancy in the Cold War. A shared commitment to antiracist, anticolonial ideals had strategic value in potentially facilitating relationships with the formerly colonized nations of Africa and Asia.

Influenced by these conditions, the Immigration and Nationality Act (also known as the Hart-Celler Act) was passed in 1965. As in years past, the Act maintained the principle of numerical restriction by specifying caps on annual immigration into the country. But in a sharp break from the 1924 laws, the Hart-Celler Act abolished the national origins quota system, thus eliminating national origins, race, or ancestry as a basis for immigration to the United States. Instead, the new laws asserted a preference system that would guide the allocation of visas for settlement. Two basic principles organized the system. The primary one was that of family reunification; the family members of U.S. citizens and permanent residents were given preference on a first-come, first-served basis, in the queue for entry to the United States. Moreover, immediate relatives, specifically spouses, children, and the parents of U.S. citizens, were not subject to numerical quotas. The other principle was that of occupational needs; those with special occupational skills, abilities, or training that were in short supply in the United States could apply to immigrate there. These two main principles—of family reunification and employment—were central to the U.S. immigration policies from this time until the end of the century when restriction and enforcement took center stage.

By lifting discriminatory national origins quotas, the 1965 Immigration and Nationality Act paved the way for the growth of a more diverse foreign-born population in the United States. As discussed in Chapter One, since the 1970s, many immigrants have been from Asia and Latin America, in contrast to the primarily European origin flows of the past. This has resulted in important shifts in the minority demographics of the country. The 2010 Census showed Latino/as to number 50.5 million (up from

35.3 million in 2000), making them the nation's largest minority group and 16.3 percent of the total population. At 37.7 million, blacks accounted for 12.2 percent and Asians for 4.7 percent (14.5 million) of the total population.[5]

The Immigration and Nationality Act and its basic principles have continued to guide U.S. immigration policy to the present day. However, spurred by a variety of conditions and interests, the Act has also been amended numerous times since its passage in 1965. Notable changes include the Refugee Act of 1980, which was passed in the aftermath of the U.S. war in Southeast Asia and the subsequent outflow of refugees from the region. The Act raised the cap on annual refugee admissions. It also adopted a definition of "refugee" based on the one created by the U.N. Convention and Protocol on the Status of Refugees, thus bringing U.S. refugee law to international standards. More generally, the 1980 Act attempted to regularize refugee policy by establishing the Office of the U.S. Coordinator for Refugee Affairs and specifying a uniform refugee resettlement and absorption policy.

In what follows we discuss some of the other developments of U.S. immigration laws during the late twentieth and early twenty-first century. The changes in the immigration system have been informed by a variety of conditions and often-conflicting interests. There is one particular issue, however—illegal immigration—that has been especially prominent in the increasingly shrill calls for stricter immigration controls that we see today.

"Secure our borders": The Era of Enforcement

The late 1970s saw the start of a rising tide of public anxiety about the flow of unauthorized immigration into the United States. Nevins (2002: 62–4) has written of the growing perception during this time, stoked by sensationalist media reports and political statements, of a crisis of unauthorized immigration. Reflecting this sense of crisis, IRCA (Immigration Reform and Control Act) was passed in 1986 after a long and arduous journey through Congress. IRCA's provisions were complex because they were reflective of compromise between divergent interest groups, from agribusiness to immigrant advocates. The Act penalized employers for knowingly hiring undocumented workers, and established a new requirement that citizenship or work eligibility be proven before the hire of a new worker. It also included what came to be known as "amnesty"—a five-year program whereby unauthorized immigrants who had been continuously present in the United States since January 1, 1982, were allowed to apply for temporary, and eventually permanent, legal status if they met certain conditions. A separate program allowed workers who had performed seasonal agricultural work (SAW) during the twelve-month period ending May 1, 1986, to legalize their status. Last but not least, IRCA mandated "enhanced border security," authorizing funds for an expansion of the apparatus of border control.

In terms of its long-term impacts, IRCA has come under fire for its inability to deter continued flows of irregular immigration into the United States, flows that actually surged in the 1990s and early 2000s. Ironically, among the reasons for the surge were the stricter U.S.-Mexico border controls that were mandated by IRCA. These controls made multiple migratory trips back and forth increasingly costly and dangerous. As a result, the once-circulating migration flows from Mexico were transformed into settlement as unauthorized immigrants remained in the United States and brought their families with them. Also of significance were the gaps in IRCA's employer deterrence system. This included the fact that employers could avoid sanctions by claims of being unaware of the irregular status of their employee (Kerwin 2010; Chishti, Meissner, and Bergeron 2011). And given the advantages of hiring undocumented workers, in terms of pay and working conditions, employers then had little incentive to stop doing so.

Indeed, as evidenced by the IRCA loopholes, the U.S. immigration regime has consistently had a Janus-faced character with respect to undocumented movements from Mexico. There has been tolerance and tacit acceptance of these movements and their presence in agriculture and other low-skilled sectors of the economy. At the same time, the regime has been driven by a sense of crisis, of the need to deter undocumented flows through punitive border control policies. Under these conditions, the punitive border control policies that arise serve only to enhance the vulnerability of immigrants.

Despite its various problems as a policy measure, IRCA was clearly successful in one respect: it achieved the regularization of millions of immigrants, giving them the opportunity to become full participants and members of U.S. society. Following the passage of IRCA, approximately 1.6 million individuals legalized their status through the general amnesty provisions, and an additional 1.1 million did so through the provisions for special agricultural workers (SAW). Those who regularized their status through IRCA were then able to sponsor qualifying relatives through regular immigration channels. The program had particular significance for Mexican immigrants who constituted an estimated 70 percent of IRCA beneficiaries (Chishti, Meissner, and Bergeron 2011). As seen below in Figure 2.0, Mexican immigration to the United States rose sharply during the closing decades of the twentieth

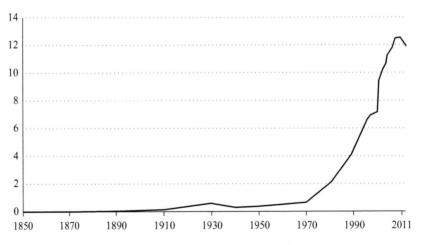

Figure 2.0   Mexican-Born Population in the U.S., 1850–2011 (in millions)

Source: 2012 Pew Research Center. "Net Migration from Mexico Falls to Zero—and Perhaps Less." http://www.pewhispanic.org/2012/04/23/ net-migration-from-mexico-falls-to-zero-and-perhaps-less/. Reprinted with permission.

century. We see this trend reversing, however, in the early 2000s. In an analysis of this decline, Passel, Cohn, and Barrera (2012) suggest several underlying factors, including a weakened U.S. job market, heightened border enforcement, and the growing Mexican economy with increasing job opportunities for its citizens.

The 1990 Immigration Act and the Immigration Preference System

The next set of major changes to U.S. immigration law occurred in 1990. As with previous laws, this set also embodied the contradiction of the expansion of opportunities for immigrant entry, particularly for highly skilled labor, alongside strictly defined categories and pushback from those who saw immigrants as taking jobs from Americans. At this time Congress raised the cap on annual immigration to the United States from 500,000 to 700,000. It also introduced the category of "Temporary Protected Status," which enabled the Attorney General to exempt from deportation those irregular immigrants who were nationals of countries suffering from armed conflict or natural disasters. A program of Diversity visas (also known as the Green Card Lottery) was introduced to provide immigration opportunities to persons from countries with low rates of immigration to the United States. Diversity visas were limited to eligible applicants from nations that did not have a cumulative total of 50,000 immigrants in the previous five years. No more than 55,000 Diversity visas were made available each fiscal year.

But perhaps the most important feature of the 1990 laws was a commitment to enhancing employment-based immigration. The Act more than doubled the number of employment-based preference visas, from 54,000 to 140,000 annually. In addition, the 1990 laws authorized an expansion of temporary employment visas, including the H-1B visa that allows U.S. employers to temporarily employ foreign workers in specialty occupations. The H-1B visa encompasses people in specialty occupations such as scientific research and information technology. Many eventually apply for permanent residence through the employment-based channels of the immigration system (Jachimowicz and Meyers 2002). In 1990, the annual number of H-1B visas was capped at 65,000. During the high-tech boom of the late 1990s, the cap was raised, from 115,000 in 1999 and 2000 and then to 195,000 during 2001–2003. Corporate leaders had lobbied for the increases, countering the efforts of H-1B restrictionists who claimed that the visas took away jobs from U.S. workers. In his 2002 testimony before the House Science and Technology Committee in March, Microsoft Chairman Bill Gates stated that the shortage of H-1B visas was leaving high-tech jobs in the United States unfilled, forcing companies to move their operations abroad and thus ultimately resulting in job losses for U.S. workers. More generally, the pro–H-1B business lobby argued for the importance of attracting highly skilled immigrants as a strategy for the United States to remain competitive in the global economy. Since 2004, however, the H-1B visa cap has reverted back to the original limit of 115,000.

Table 2.0 provides percentage breakdowns by class of admission, of those granted permanent residence in the United States from 1990 to 2010. We see that those coming in as immediate relatives of U.S. citizens have consistently formed a major portion of admissions, especially since the mid-1990s. The data also suggest that the 1990 Act had a positive impact on employment-based admissions. In 1991, 3.3 percent of those gaining legal permanent residence came in under employment-based preferences, a percentage that rose to 11.9 percent in 1992. At the same time, we also see that with the exception of the year 2005, the percentage of those coming under family-sponsored preferences has consistently outstripped that of employment-based preferences.

The principle of family reunification, established in 1965, has thus remained a primary feature of the U.S. immigration system. The 1990 Immigration Act, however, with its focus on increasing employment as a basis of admission to the United States, reflects growing concerns about the ability of a system that is based on humanitarian concerns to attract "the best and the brightest." Informed by a global neoliberal regime, the contemporary era has been one driven less by family values and more by notions of a

Table 2.0: Legal Permanent Residence by Class of Admission, 1990–2010

Year	% Immediate Relatives of U.S Citizens	% Family-Sponsored Preferences	% Employ-ment-based preferences	% Refugees/ Asylees	Other Immi-grants
1990	15.1%	14.0%	3.8%	6.3%	60.8%
1991	13.0%	11.8%	3.3%	7.6%	64.3%
1992	24.2%	21.9%	11.9%	12.0%	30.0%
1993	28.2%	25.1%	16.2%	14.1%	16.4%
1994	31.1%	26.3%	15.3%	15.1%	12.2%
1995	30.6%	33.1%	11.8%	15.9%	8.6%
1996	32.9%	32.1%	12.8%	14.0%	8.2%
1997	40.2%	26.7%	11.4%	14.0%	7.7%
1998	43.3%	29.3%	11.8%	8.0%	7.6%
1999	40.0%	33.6%	8.8%	6.6%	11.0%
2000	41.2%	28.0%	12.7%	7.4%	10.7%
2001	41.6%	21.9%	16.9%	10.2%	9.4%
2002	45.7%	17.6%	16.4%	11.9%	8.4%
2003	47.0%	22.6%	11.6%	6.4%	12.4%
2004	43.6%	22.4%	16.2%	7.4%	10.4%
2005	38.9%	19.0%	22.0%	12.7%	7.4%
2006	45.8%	17.5%	12.6%	17.1%	7.0%
2007	47.0%	18.6%	15.4%	12.9%	6.1%
2008	44.1%	20.7%	15.0%	15.0%	5.2%
2009	47.4%	18.7%	12.7%	15.7%	5.5%
2010	45.7%	20.6%	14.2%	13.1%	6.4%

Source: U.S. Department of Homeland Security, Office of Immigration Statistics, *Yearbook of Immigration Statistics* (various years). http://www.dhs. gov/ximgtn/statistics/publications/yearbook.shtm

"global professional immigrant market" in which nations compete for the most favorable contenders, in terms of their human capital.

IIRIRA (Illegal Immigration Reform and Immigrant Responsibility Act) and the USA Patriot Act

The 1990 Act was followed by rising anti-immigrant sentiment and the passage of a series of measures that aimed for stricter immigration enforcement. Fueling these trends was the economic recession of the early 1990s along with a widespread perception of the failure of past immigration policies, specifically IRCA's inadequacy as a deterrence program. These grievances became especially apparent in California, which passed Proposition 187 with 59 percent of the popular vote in 1994. Prop 187 was a state law that would have denied virtually all public services to irregular immigrants and their children. It was, however, never actually implemented and was eventually struck down as unconstitutional. Between 1993 and 1996 the Immigration and Naturalization Service (INS) budget, especially that directed toward border control, rose by 68 percent (DeSipio and de la Garza 1998). Additionally, 1994 saw the launch of Operation Gatekeeper, an intensive border control program in San Diego, California that aimed to stop unauthorized movements across the U.S.-Mexico border. In his study of Operation Gatekeeper, Nevins (2002) writes of how such government programs did not just reflect a public perception of an illegal immigration crisis, but also helped to create it:

> The state did not simply respond to public concern with the supposed crisis of "illegal" immigration. Rather, it has helped to create the "illegal" through the construction of the boundary and the expansion of the INS's enforcement capacity. The state also played a significant role in creating the putative crisis posed by "illegals" through the rhetoric it employed to justify its efforts to bring order to the U.S.-Mexico boundary and to rid U.S. territory of those without state sanction to be within its boundaries . . . the category of "illegal" proved extremely useful in mobilizing public support for enhanced boundary and immigration enforcement. (11)

The campaign to "secure our borders" moved ahead in 1996 with the passage of the Illegal Immigration Reform and Immigrant Responsibility Act (IIRIRA). In conjunction with the 1996 Personal Responsibility and Work Opportunity Reconciliation Act, IIRIRA reduced immigrant access to social safety-net programs. It increased border personnel, authorized construction of further barriers on the Mexican border and stiffened penalties for various immigration offenses. It also toughened deportation procedures and tightened the rules for the sponsorship (for U.S. permanent residence) of family members by citizens of the

United States. The Antiterrorism and Effective Death Penalty Act (AEDPA) of 1996 further increased the enforcement authority of the federal government by limiting judicial review for most categories of immigrants subject to deportation. In short, the last decade of the twentieth century saw the growing criminalization of irregular migration through increasingly punitive enforcement measures.

These trends were only magnified in the aftermath of the terrorist attacks of September 11, 2001. The 9/11 attacks were followed by intense popular backlash toward those assumed to be from religious and national backgrounds similar to those of the terrorists (Cainkar 2004; Peek 2005). In the aftermath of the attacks, those who looked Middle Eastern or who had Arabic or Islamic-sounding names experienced hate crimes and bias incidents. Muslim Americans reported increased hostility as well as discrimination in the workplace on the basis of their religion (Council on American-Islamic Relations 2008).

Popular antipathy toward Muslims was bolstered by many of the post 9/11 policy initiatives taken by the U.S. government. Even if inadvertently, these policies strengthened popular stereotypes and images that associated terrorism with Muslims. A month after the 9/11 attacks, George W. Bush approved the USA Patriot Act, which gave expanded legal powers to government agencies to implement special measures to address terrorism, both domestically and abroad. These measures included a special registration program in 2002 for noncitizen men aged sixteen to sixty-four from selected countries—Eritrea, North Korea, and twenty-three Muslim-majority states. The program required these persons to register with the U.S. immigration authorities and to undergo interviews with them.

The special registration program was phased out in 2003, but the U.S. government's use of "extraordinary measures" to monitor and in some cases to remove noncitizen immigrants deemed possible threats to national security continued throughout the decade. The Patriot Act allowed for immigrants who were not citizens to be arrested on alleged suspicion, to be secretly and indefinitely detained, and also to be forcibly deported. For the purposes of protecting national security interests, the Act also authorized government agencies to use surveillance and wiretapping without showing probable cause, and to secretly obtain and search private records and property. These developments did not, however, go without protest. Especially affected by these measures, Middle Eastern and Muslim American organizations mobilized court challenges and public demonstrations against them (Bakalian and Bozorgmehr 2009).

The U.S. government's War on Terror was accompanied by the reorganization and expansion of government agencies responsible for immigration control. The fact that the attacks were carried out by foreign nationals who had come to the United States on student and visitor visas placed a spotlight on the efficiency of immigration and border control agencies. In 2003, the newly created Department of Homeland Security (DHS) streamlined the previous immigration and border control responsibilities of the Immigration and Naturalization Service, elevating government capacity and authority to carry out federal policies and programs. DHS, in turn, created the Bureau of Immigration and Customs Enforcement (ICE), a new agency dedicated to apprehending, detaining, and deporting "criminal and fugitive" noncitizens (Kanstroom 2007). ICE launched a series of programs in collaboration with state and local agencies. These included the Criminal Alien Program (CAP), which placed ICE officials at state prisons to conduct immigrant screening, and the Secure Communities Program, which relied on police to enter prints of arrestees into a joint FBI and ICE database.

The opening decades of the twenty-first century thus saw a vast expansion of the state apparatus of immigration control. This trend, which had been evident in the 1990s, grew further in the aftermath of 9/11 when immigration control became a major security issue. But even with these changes, those in favor of stricter immigration controls remained unsatisfied and pushed for more enforcement procedures. Many of these additional laws, even when approved by legislative bodies, faced legal challenges and so remained stalled at the implementation stage. Nonetheless, we would argue that as a call to further action, they had enormous significance for the political discourse of immigration in the United

States. In conjunction with the expansion of the government apparatus of immigration control, they legitimized public resentment and hostility toward unauthorized immigrants, positioning them as "bad immigrants" in the good immigrant–bad immigrant dichotomy.

In 2005 Congress passed the REAL ID Act, which required states to verify U.S. citizenship or permanent residence before issuing drivers' licenses and identification cards. Implementation of the Act was delayed, as many states resisted it on both cost and privacy grounds. At the same time, several states passed their own "get tough on illegal immigration" bills. These included Arizona's infamous Senate Bill 1070. Passed in 2010, the bill expanded the powers of state police officers to ask about the immigration status of anyone they stopped, and to hold in police custody those suspected of being illegal immigrants. The legislation required police officers, "when practicable," to detain people whom they reasonably suspected to be in the country without papers and to verify their status with federal officials. SB 1070 also made it a state crime—a misdemeanor—to not carry immigration papers. In addition, it allowed people to sue local government or agencies if they believed that these institutions were not enforcing federal or state immigration laws. After its passage, SB 1070 was challenged and the federal courts suspended many of its provisions.

The Deportation Regime and Immigrant Rights Movement

In the lives of U.S. immigrants, especially those who are undocumented, the era of enforcement has produced a climate of fear and vulnerability. Nicholas de Genova (2005) has argued that these experiences emerge in relation to a deportation regime. These are conditions in which the state uses policing and surveillance, along with the constant threat of deportation, to discipline undocumented immigrants such as to ensure their compliance and passivity. The powerful experience of deportability that results for the immigrant is also complicated by its many layers. Even as the undocumented immigrant is officially illegal, she is also accepted and perhaps even welcomed at certain times and situations, such as at her workplace (Coutin 2005; Menjívar 2006). The fluidity and contradictions of legal and illegal status are vividly highlighted by Roberto Gonzalez's (2011) study of undocumented youth who came to the United States as children. For them, the transition into adulthood was accompanied by a transition into illegality. As children, they were able to attend school, protected from the direct arm of the deportation regime by the Family Educational Rights and Privacy Act, which prevents schools from releasing student records to immigration authorities. But after finishing high school they found themselves in a very different legal space, one in which their deportability loomed large and they were prohibited from legal employment.

If the deportation regime is an especially powerful structure in the lives of the undocumented, its impacts extend well beyond them. The surveillance and policing that have been part of the era of enforcement also come to shadow the lives of those who are under suspicion of being undocumented. Since being undocumented does not carry an immediately visible marker, what the authorities turn to instead are proxies. "Racial Profiling" refers to the discriminatory practice by law enforcement officials of targeting individuals for suspicion of crime based on the individual's race, ethnicity, religion, or national origin. Latino/as have been especially likely to be under suspicion of being undocumented. Figure 2.1 reveals the gradual increase in deportations over the past ten years in the United States.

The deportation regime has not, however, gone without protest. The era of immigration enforcement has generated a climate of fear and anxiety for immigrants, but it has also spurred some to political action. Immigrants have mobilized to challenge and protest various features of the U.S. immigration regime. The growth of an immigrant rights movement that is particularly focused on the plight of unauthorized immigrants became visible in 2006. In the spring of that year, massive political demonstrations took place across the country in what organizers described as a "national day of action for immigration justice." The protests had first developed in response to the Sensenbrenner Bill, which would have made the mere status of being an undocumented

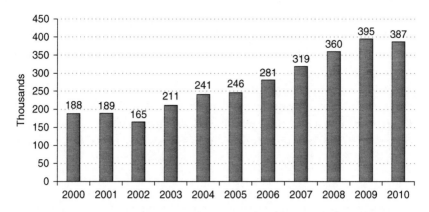

Figure 2.1 Removals of Undocumented Immigrants, 2000–2010[6]

Source: 2011 Pew Research Center. As Deportations Rise to Record Levels, Most Latinos Oppose Obama's Policy. http://www.pewhispanic. org/2011/12/28/as-deportations-rise-to-record-levels-most-latinos-oppose-obamas-policy/. Reprinted with permission.

immigrant a felony subject to imprisonment as well as deportation from the United States. The protests continued after the bill was successfully blocked. Calling themselves the "new civil rights movement," protest leaders articulated broader goals of justice and humane treatment for undocumented immigrants. They successfully mobilized a broad coalition of support, drawing on churches, labor unions, student organizations, and a variety of other progressive groups. In their analysis of the "Spring Marches of 2006," Pantoja, Menjívar, and Magaña (2009) note how these protests gave visibility and voice to undocumented immigrants, bringing them "out of the shadows" and into the political spotlight. Holding placards that said, "I am not illegal, I am human" or "No human being is illegal," participants of the marches protested the dehumanizing images of illegal immigrants in popular culture and discourse (Summers Sandoval 2008). In August of 2012, about thirty-six undocumented immigrants embarked on a six-week bus ride across the Southern states to the 2012 Democratic National Convention in North Carolina. The "UndocuBus" participants aimed to confront the fear and humiliation surrounding their experience. The words on the side of the bus "No Papers, No Fear" openly identified the protestors as they drove. They took their issue directly to the Democratic National Convention in order to bring attention to the lack of political action, and to emphasize the urgency of this issue to President Obama.[7] Without the right to vote, these immigrants have been determined to find other avenues of political participation. Despite the culture of fear resulting from the deportation regime, these restrictive laws have ignited many to fight for immigrant rights and justice.

Comprehensive Immigration Reform: "Good" and "Bad" Immigrants in Key Debates

The early twenty-first century was thus a time of important advancement for the immigrant rights movement in the United States. However, as of 2012, a central goal of the movement—to achieve a far-reaching overhaul of the U.S. immigration regime—had not been achieved. In 2006 and 2007 Congress took up "comprehensive immigration reform" bills that combined strategies of immigration enforcement, legalization, and changes to the visa system, but no agreement was reached. With Comprehensive Immigration Reform on the agenda for President Obama's second term in office, the goal will be to overcome the past and current deadlock between divergent interests to develop a unified plan to fix the system.

Calls for Comprehensive Immigration Reform (CIR) come from businesses, policymakers, and organizations representing a variety of distinct interests, including labor organizations, business owners, and immigrant rights advocates. The pro-CIR movement can be divided into two distinct political camps that use "good" and "bad" immigrant tropes to frame calls for reform: Immigration Pragmatists (IP) and Immigration Advocates (IA). While Immigration Pragmatists manipulate "good" and "bad" images to discern which immigrants are necessary for America's growth as a superpower and which are expendable or prohibited, advocates tend to highlight "good" images of immigrants' contributions to American society and their capabilities of assimilating to American values. The lack of solidarity in the pro-CIR movement is evident in recent prominent and controversial policy debates over issues such as the STEM Jobs Act and E-Verify Exemptions. Although both IP and IA groups desire immigration reform (in contrast to Immigration Restrictionists (IR) who oppose reform), their goals are so sharply different that they often come up short in developing a comprehensive plan.

We define Immigration Pragmatists as groups, organizations, and policymakers who emphasize neoliberal ideals in order to find a middle ground between valorizing and vilifying immigrants. Among those of the pro-CIR platform, Pragmatists most often juxtapose "good" and "bad" images of immigrants in political debates in order to justify why some groups of immigrants have more value than others. Often, IP groups argue for immigration reform and legislation that benefit special interest groups, corporations, and U.S. consumers. While typically on the Republican Right, Pragmatists tend to avoid the hard-line cuts to immigration numbers across the board proposed by Immigration Restrictionists who lead the anti-CIR lobby. Instead, IP groups use "good" and "bad" immigrant tropes to pick and choose which groups will contribute to America's continued status as a global economic superpower. By manipulating these images, Pragmatists attempt to avoid criticism for continuing to employ foreign workers despite high rates of U.S. unemployment. In the course of U.S. history, IP groups have been influential in supporting guest worker initiatives such as the Bracero Program, as well as policies to increase the distribution of visas to high-skilled immigrants. Rather than a blanket endorsement of all immigrants, Pragmatists often advocate specifically for those who appear to meet business interests (Dietrich 2012: 738).

The issue of increasing high-skilled immigrant visas and specifically, the proposed STEM Jobs Act (Science, Technology, Engineering, and Math), offers an example of a political debate in which the rhetoric of "good" and "bad" immigrants has been quite visible. Answering the call to retain and attract high-skilled immigrants in the STEM fields, the STEM Jobs Act (H.R. 6429) of 2012 was proposed by Judiciary Committee Chairman Lamar

Smith (R). The proposal was to reallocate the 55,000 green cards available through the Diversity Visa Lottery to foreign graduates from U.S. universities with advanced STEM degrees (Smith 2012). Anti-CIR Restrictionists oppose the bill, arguing that it would generate more competition for highly skilled American workers, and also allow sponsorship for the low-skilled family members of these immigrants to come to the United States. Immigration Pragmatists and Advocates have had a different response to the STEM Jobs Act. Immigration Pragmatists support this bill as they see it as beneficial for the economy, but caution against the migration of family members beyond the high-skilled visa recipients. Organizations and think tanks taking the IP stance praise the removal of the Diversity Visa Lottery and warn against the STEM Jobs Act clause allowing spouses and children of legal permanent residents admission to the United States during green card processing. One of their fears is that the family recruits will add to the less-desirable population who will rely on government resources. While there is no explicit racism detectable in this argument, the targeting of the low-skilled as undesirable immigrants reflects an ordering of humans that basically states those who are less educated are less worthy. Again, this suggests that the Immigration Pragmatist standpoint is not to do away with immigration, but rather to bring "good immigrants only" to strengthen the United States as a global superpower.

While Immigrant Advocates support the Pro-CIR proposal to provide visas to high-skilled immigrants, they disagree that the STEM visas should replace the existing Diversity Visa Lottery. The calls of Immigration Pragmatists to limit the potential for chain migration produced by STEM visas has also been a source of disagreement among those potential supporters of a comprehensive reform bill. Citing a 2012 report by the Information Technology Industry Council, the Partnership for a New American Economy, and the U.S. Chamber of Commerce, the Massachusetts Immigrant and Refugee Advocacy Coalition explains:

> Immigrant STEM workers, in short, don't "take American jobs"—they help build them. . . . We endorse these calls, with one critical caveat:

expansion of visas for skilled immigrants should not come at the expense of diversity visas or the traditional emphasis on family reunification, a feature of some of the proposed bills. This is not just a matter of equity: some of the same research cited above testifies to the economic contributions of immigrants at all levels of the U.S. workforce—not least in high-growth health care occupations. (Gross 2012)

Immigration Advocates challenge the IR rhetoric by counteracting the idea that immigrants take jobs by putting forth a narrative of "good" immigrants that create jobs. In a departure from IP claims that high-skilled visas should replace diversity lotteries and that there should be measures to curb the migration of low-skilled persons, IA groups highlight the work ethic of immigrants as well as the importance of family reunification as an American cultural principle in their calls for immigration reform. Ultimately, President Obama expressed opposition to the proposed STEM Jobs Act, citing his disagreement with the narrowness of the proposed reform, particularly the limits on visas for family members and the removal of the Diversity Visa program.[8]

In addition to debates about visas for the highly skilled, another hot topic in Comprehensive Immigration Reform has been the continued employment of undocumented immigrants by U.S. business owners. For Immigration Restrictionists, the depiction of illegal aliens as "bad" immigrants stealing jobs from deserving Americans has been particularly effective for organizing enforcement efforts to punish employers and the undocumented immigrants who work for them. In the early twenty-first century, a federal program called E-Verify has been proposed to stem the hiring of undocumented immigrants. Before the establishment of an electronic verification system for confirming the authorization of workers, companies were able to feign ignorance of the status of employees. IR proponents of E-Verify support the use of the program to not only reduce numbers of "bad immigrants" but to also chastise their employers. Neglecting the many contributions of immigrants to the United States, IR rhetoric emphasizes immigrants as dangerous criminals who hurt rather than help the United States:

The groups who oppose E-Verify do so because it works. Agriculture groups wish to continue employing illegal workers at a lower cost than U.S. citizens. However, they refuse to understand they are leaving Americans out of work in a time of high unemployment and providing cover and financing to transnational criminals and potential terrorists. (FAIR 2013)

While many hard-line Immigration Restrictionists applaud mandatory E-Verify implementation for businesses, Pro-CIR groups tend to react differently to the program. In their opposition to the E-Verify legislation, both Immigrants Advocates and Immigration Pragmatists emphasize its potential negative impacts on "good" legal immigrants, U.S. citizens and businesses. They identify potential problems of identity fraud as well as the costs for businesses and employers to implement the system and to replace workers who may be fired as a result of nonconfirmation through the E-Verify system. Also cited is the possible loss of the revenues generated by payroll taxes from undocumented workers who may begin to work "off the books" as a result of E-Verify (Fuller 2011; Rosenblum & Hoyt 2011; Wolgin 2011).

The political response to mandatory E-Verify has included demands that certain industries, specifically agriculture and domestic work, remain exempt from its requirements. While for Immigration Pragmatists these demands may be legitimized on instrumental grounds, for Immigration Restrictionists there can be no exceptions to the rule that employers be held accountable for the hiring of undocumented immigrant labor. Immigrant Advocates have focused on the issue of what the exemption implies for the continued exploitation of domestic and agricultural workers and their families. Groups supporting domestic workers' rights have cited the E-verify exemption to domestic work in their efforts to push for recognition of domestic work in fair labor laws. In doing so they have drawn on the imagery of "good immigrant workers" who are doing the crucial work of keeping American families afloat.

There is little doubt that the single most controversial feature of Comprehensive Immigration Reform proposals has been that of legalization. In an era in which the illegal immigrant has been a particular target of nativist rhetoric, the idea of legalization has been an extremely controversial one. Under these conditions, immigrant rights advocates have focused their activism on a segment of the undocumented population that evokes the least controversy. These are unauthorized persons who came to the United States as children. Their circumstances disrupt the nativist imagery of the illegal immigrant as a self-conscious criminal. Rather, cultural notions of childhood innocence reinforce the idea that these persons are legitimate beneficiaries of legalization since they are unauthorized through no fault of their own.

The Development, Relief, and Education for Alien Minors (DREAM) Act was proposed in 2010 to grant legal status to certain unauthorized immigrants who entered the United States as children and had completed specified higher education or military service requirements (Chishti and Hipsman 2012). The Republican-controlled Senate ultimately blocked the bill. The issues of the DREAM Act received political attention once again in June 2012, however, when President Obama issued a directive to grant deferred legal action to certain unauthorized immigrants who were brought to the United States as children. While the directive did not guarantee citizenship or provide "amnesty," eligible individuals were able to request temporary relief from deportation proceedings and to apply for work authorization and drivers' licenses. To be decided on a case-by-case basis, the directive was also only to apply to those who met certain conditions, such as entering the United States before the age of sixteen, being enrolled in school, and having no criminal record.[9] The Migration Policy Institute (MPI)[10] estimated that up to 1.4 million people would qualify for relief under the terms of the directive, which was strongly supported by Latino/as.[11] With President Obama's re-election in 2012, many speculate that the DREAM Act will be included in the agenda for comprehensive immigration reform. Additionally, public opinion about undocumented immigrants appears to be shifting. In an exit poll from the 2012 presidential election, when asked about immigration, "Less than 3 in 10 voters said that most illegal immigrants working in the United States should be deported, while nearly two-thirds said such people should be offered a chance to apply for legal status."[12]

Nativism and Race in the Era of Enforcement

The late twentieth and early twenty-first century era of immigration enforcement has been closely accompanied by the rise of a powerful nativist movement. The nativism of today draws on longstanding themes of protecting the American nation from infiltration by undesirable, unassimilable, and indeed violent foreign elements. But in accordance with color-blind racial ideology, contemporary nativism does not explicitly invoke race as a basis for exclusion from the United States. Instead, contemporary nativism has focused on the production of images of threat, specifically that of the illegal alien and the terrorist alien.

Historian Mae Ngai (2004) has famously described the illegal alien as an " 'impossible subject' . . . a person who cannot be and a problem that cannot be solved" (4–5). The dehumanizing effects of the illegal alien label stem in part from its ability to reduce those who fall into it to a single dimension. Thus those who are unauthorized are assumed to be criminals in general, engaged in a wide range of illegal activities. They have a natural inclination to criminality, one that is moreover not simply an individual failing, but a reflection of their origins and culture. Illegality then becomes a mechanism of racialization, as it is used to condemn entire groups, imputing natural difference and inferiority to them.

In the United States, it is Latino/as and especially Mexican Americans who have been the target of the illegal alien label. With Mexico often being treated as a "special case" in U.S. immigration policies, as noted earlier, Mexican immigrants have encountered "an especially adverse context of reception in comparison to other immigrant groups" (Telles and Ortiz 2008: 286). As Mary Romero writes, "Concern over immigration to the U.S. is inseparable from stereotyping Mexicans as illegal aliens and as criminal, foreign and the other" (2008: 28). Illegality becomes a singular lens by which to look at Mexican Americans and to see them as naturally different and inferior from other Americans. Under its distorted gaze, a variety of conditions and circumstances can be taken as evidence of illegality. In *Entitled to Nothing*, Lisa Park analyzes the late 1990s California campaign against prenatal care services for immigrant mothers. She noted how a generalized notion of illegality informed the campaign, which portrayed immigrant women as having a propensity for fraud and unethically "'working' the system by having children and therefore undeserving of social services for themselves or their children" (2011:15).

Along with the "illegal alien" focus of immigration control, the notion of a "terrorist alien" has also developed. In reality, the boundaries between the two are not clear, as each may be evoked in concert with the other during processes of stigmatization. As we have described, in the aftermath of 9/11, Middle Eastern and Muslim Americans have been especially vulnerable to the charge of "terrorist alien," a particular target of immigration control efforts that are focused on terrorism threats. The label has served as a mechanism of their racialization—of a widespread attribution to them of naturalized inferiority. That is, reflecting their origins and culture, they have a natural inclination toward violence and terrorism.

The images of the "illegal alien" and "terrorist alien" have also been part of contemporary constructions of the "bad immigrant." Again, we argue that the bad immigrant's counterpoint of the good immigrant is emblematic of the values of the neoliberal global regime. The image is of professionals or highly skilled workers who represent a net gain for the United States in terms of human capital in the competitive global economy. He or she is entrepreneurial and self-sufficient—unlikely to make demands on a declining system of government safety nets and supports. The good immigrant then stands as an effective counterpoint to the bad immigrant. The condemnation of illegal aliens draws legitimacy from it. Those who portray unauthorized immigrants in dehumanizing ways and advocate punitive measures against them can simultaneously proclaim that they are not anti-immigrant or racist. It is just those immigrants who are unauthorized—defined by their illegality—who are the focus of their ire.

Conclusions: Immigration Policy and Racial Formation

Immigration policy and its developments are nation-building processes. It is a sphere in which questions of national culture, interests, and membership are negotiated and institutionalized. As we have seen in the course of this chapter, the debates and resulting policy outcomes are highly contested, reflecting deep divisions of society around these questions.

By their very nature, these issues are enmeshed in, and indeed inseparable from, the dynamics of the racial order. Thus, as we have seen, prevailing ideologies of scientific racism informed the passage of the 1924 National Origins Act, which attempted to restrict immigration to those coming from northern and western Europe. 1965 brought a shift away from these policies as the United States began to embrace the ideals of a "color-blind" society. Today we see the trace of race in immigration policy in more subtle and less clearly visible ways, intertwined as it is with notions of criminality and threats to national security.

But immigration policy has not just reflected the racial order; it has also shaped it. One way it does this is in how it influences the demographics of the country, which then change the context in which racial identities and boundaries are formulated and negotiated. For example, as analysts often mention, the 1965 Act opened the doors to a wide range of people from Africa, Asia, and Latin America, thereby changing the terrain on which race is negotiated. The black-white division, historically the central axis of race in the United States, has been called into question with these new groups who do not neatly fit into pre-existing categories. Also, the political debates of immigration have shaped racial discourse and ideologies. Among the most powerful consequences of the 1924 Act was how it brought scientific racism's vocabulary and concepts into popular culture. In the contemporary era, an increasingly punitive and visible immigration regime has served to racialize targeted groups. The institutional structure and practices of immigration, including those related to surveillance and control, also have consequences for the racial order.

As we have seen throughout this chapter, the history of U.S. immigration policy reveals an ongoing dialectic of labor market demands and nativism. We see an ongoing cycle in which these intersecting forces shape the development of immigration policy, which in turn informs the racialization of immigrant groups. Telles and Ortiz have described this cycle in their analysis of the Mexican American experience: "American capitalists' desire to quench its persistent thirst for cheap Mexican labor for a century, which is supported by the American state and enabled by Mexico's proximity and its large labor supply, can largely account for the persistent low status and ethnic retention of Mexican Americans" (2008: 285).

The active recruitment of labor from abroad is an integral part of U.S. history. In the next chapter we will explore immigrant experiences in the labor market, focusing on the relationship of these experiences to the race–immigration nexus.

3

Race and the Occupational Strategies of Immigrants

Mexican immigrant gardeners, Vietnamese immigrant manicurists, West Indian immigrant caregivers. As suggested by these popular images, occupations are an important part of the racialization of immigrants—of their incorporation into the U.S. racial order. In this chapter we explore the occupational strategies of immigrants in the contemporary United States. We consider some of the many ways in which immigrants strive to make a living and to improve their circumstances in the labor market. The occupational opportunities and strategies of immigrants, as we will see, offer a powerful lens on the race–immigration nexus. As immigrants strategize to enhance their situation, they simultaneously negotiate the racial order and their place within it.

In our analysis of immigrant occupational strategies, we draw on theories of immigrant incorporation that highlight the role of larger social, economic, and political conditions in shaping the immigrant experience. Our analytic path thus takes us away from neoclassical economics, including human capital theories, which have often guided the study of the labor market incorporation of immigrants. In brief, these theories focus on the "human capital" of immigrants as measured by such variables as levels of education, occupational skills, and competence in the language of the receiving society. This neat equation asserts that these characteristics are then reflected in the labor market location of immigrants, with higher levels of human capital reflected in better labor market outcomes. From this perspective, the occupational strategies of immigrants are best understood as individual efforts to maximize their own levels of human capital in order to gain a more favorable position in the labor market. Though the individual efforts and abilities of immigrants play varying roles in their economic positions, we find that their experiences cannot be fully explained from this perspective. The levels of education, occupational skills, and language capabilities of immigrants need to be evaluated in relation to the structures of inequality that surround them: particularly the racial order, the composition of immigrant families and networks, the historical and political context of the sending country and its relationship to the United States, the organization of ethnic niches, and the dynamics of the dual labor market, which filters immigrants into specific occupations that often do not align with their human capital.

In our analysis of immigrants in the U.S. labor market, we focus on how immigrants strategize in relation to these broad social, political, and economic conditions. As described in Chapter One, immigrant groups are often disproportionately working in particular jobs or employment niches. We devote considerable attention to the formation of ethnic niches as both a strategy of ethnic groups to find employment and to respond to discrimination in the labor market. These niches, with their constantly evolving boundaries, may be local, national, or global in scope, encompassing a variety of markets. Additionally, racial imagery, both overt and cloaked in color-blind "cultural" rhetoric, infuses the recruitment, hiring, and treatment of immigrants. We see this in a wide variety of contexts, from the recruitment efforts of companies that seek nurses from abroad to work in the United States, to the preference for immigrant labor that is often expressed by employers of low-waged workers. To move beyond a generic discussion of ethnic niches, we use the term "occupational racialization" to refer to the fluid and contested processes by which particular jobs or occupational areas acquire racial meaning and significance. We also suggest that occupational racialization has been a core feature of immigrant incorporation into U.S. society.

Despite the illusion of agency, the creation and maintenance of niches reflects a complex configuration of factors, ranging from the history of relations between sending and receiving societies to the operation of social networks among immigrants that provide information and entrée to jobs. As these conditions take shape, both the occupation and the immigrant group take on racial meanings. These meanings work to naturalize the character and temperament of the immigrants and their association with the particular job in question. As a result, they are seen as intrinsically suited for the job. A large body of research has documented the role played by group stereotypes in employer recruitment practices. Maldonado (2009: 1018) writes: "Racial meanings inform and affect employers' perception and evaluations of workers, their judgment regarding which workers are fit for different jobs, their assessment of who are good and bad workers, the production of notions of skill, the connection of skills to specific jobs and the production of meanings about jobs themselves." By viewing occupations through the race–immigration nexus, we begin to understand how racialized and gendered niches channel immigrants into particular occupations producing divergent consequences for immigrants and their identity formations. While human capital is implicated in labor market strategies, we need to look beyond these attributes to fully understand the obstacles immigrants face as they integrate into American society.

Ethnic Niches and Racial Formation

Underlying the occupational strategies of immigrants are "ethnic niche" dynamics. We define "ethnic niche" as an ongoing social formation that is characterized by the clustering of an ethnic group in a particular occupation or industry, whether as workers and/ or owners. While ethnic niches may involve immigrant and non-immigrant co-ethnics (such as immigrant Italians and U.S.-born Italians), the former typically play a key role in the maintenance of the niche.

As mentioned in Chapter One, ethnicity, in contrast to race, is often associated with a choice made by the members of a group based on the belief that they have ties to each other (Cornell and

Hartmann 1998: 17). This belief plays into the formation and evolution of niches. Ethnic identities are not always a choice, however; they can also be assigned by others. We see this tension appear in the formation of ethnic niches. Among the notable features of ethnic niches is their constantly evolving character. While niches may, for example, change in their market scope, in terms of the regions in which they are located, the breadth of their clientele, and the range of offered services, these shifts often do not remove the immutable characteristics attached to certain ethnic niches. The history of the Vietnamese niche in the nail-care industry offers a fascinating example of these processes in action. The niche first formed in California in the late 1970s when many Vietnamese refugees came to the United States. Because these newly arrived immigrants did not need strong English skills or a large amount of money to start a nail-care business, the number of such businesses quickly increased. Since then nail care has expanded across the country and indeed into global markets. This expansion has been concomitant with "niche stretching" or "a broadening [of] the customer base for professional nail care and [a] deepening and diversifying [of] the range of nail-care offerings" (Eckstein and Nguyen 2011: 653). By making nail-care services affordable and easily accessible, the niche has served to expand the customer base for professional manicures from a small, elite segment of women to a larger clientele of women from diverse class and ethnic backgrounds. Over time, the nail-care business has also expanded to include not just manicures but a wider range of services such as pedicures and hair removal (Kang 2010). Although these types of changes offer important opportunities to those involved, the notion that Asian immigrant women are naturally suited to perform these services persists.

Besides market scope, ethnic niches can also shift in their collective identities—in the ethnic boundaries that constitute the niche. Ethnic niches may, for example, expand to accommodate a wider range of groups and subgroups in their base of workers and/or owners. For example, since the mid-twentieth century Mexican immigrants have formed an important labor niche in

U.S. agriculture. But over time this labor niche has diversified to include a wider range of Latino/a immigrant groups. Since the 1980s, the United States has seen an influx of Central Americans, many fleeing the ravages of military campaigns and conflicts in the region. What first began as a specifically Mexican immigrant niche has thus expanded over time to include immigrants from Guatemala and El Salvador. In these circumstances, as we will further explore in Chapter Four, the niche may become an important arena in the formation of new identities.

Perhaps the best-known aspect of ethnic niche change is that of "ethnic succession." This is a process whereby one ethnic group replaces another one in the occupational niche, often accompanied by other shifts in the character of the niche as well. In a flourishing economy, succession occurs when "the shape of the queue tightens the supply of established groups; applications from the members of incumbents' core network fall off; lower-ranked groups then get pulled up the totem pole, replacing previously established groups with little or no conflict" (Waldinger 1999: 307–8). Although ethnic succession occurs in both high- and low-skilled occupations, most movement occurs at the bottom of the labor market. Increased exposure to other occupations with higher pay and benefits often entices immigrants to seek employment outside the established niche. Movement out of an ethnic niche is particularly prominent for members of the second generation. In a *New York Times* article titled "Diners in Changing Hands; Greek Ownership on the Wane," Berger (2008)[1] describes the ongoing decline of Greek-owned diners, a staple of the New York, New Jersey, and Connecticut regions since the mid-twentieth century. The article profiles Mr. Karkambasis, a Greek immigrant and owner of the Yorktown Coach Diner. After arriving in New York City from Sparta, Greece, in 1968, Mr. Karkambasis had worked in diners, as a dishwasher, busboy, short-order cook, and waiter. He eventually accumulated enough money and knowledge of the business to buy his own diner. Like many other Greek diner owners, he spoke of how his own children had moved into white-collar jobs and were not interested in taking over the business. Moreover, the institution of the local diner was itself under threat from franchise restaurants. Under these conditions, processes of ethnic succession were evident, along with changes in the character of these establishments:

> Mr. Karkambasis, like many others in the business, foresees the end of a chapter in American restaurant history—the ownership of a large share of diners by Greek immigrants. The Park View Diner in Fairview was sold roughly six months ago to Korean owners. The Broadway Diner, a streamlined and Hopperesque throwback in Yonkers, is now owned by an immigrant from Bangladesh. The Parkside Diner in Yonkers was rebuilt a year ago as part of the homespun Malecon chain of four Dominican chicken and rice-and-beans restaurants.

Alternatively, during periods of economic downturn, competition between groups may arise, preventing easy succession. An ethnic group occupying a stable, well-paying occupational niche may work to hire co-ethnics and justify the exclusion of other ethnic groups. These efforts to exclude may not be overtly racist, but they can nevertheless serve to racialize niches by using hiring practices that disadvantage other groups. This point is highlighted by court cases over minority access to civil service positions and promotions:[2] "associations of black and Hispanic police officers have criticized psychological tests used in screening for their supposed racial biases; while an adverse selection effect is clearly visible, the deficiency in the test mechanism is more difficult to discern" (Waldinger 1999: 305). Moreover, depending on the ethnic group's position in the racial hierarchy and the nature of occupational racialization, certain immigrant groups have easier paths of succession than others.

In what follows we continue to explore the development and character of ethnic niches as features of the occupational strategies of immigrants. In doing so, we consider several different perspectives on the labor market incorporation of immigrants—social networks, state sponsorship, dual labor markets, and ethnic businesses. Drawing on these frameworks, we look at ethnic niches as arenas of racial formation. That is, we look at how developments of ethnic niches are intertwined with those of the racial order.

Social Networks and the Formation of Ethnic Niches

The construction of immigrant networks is an interactional process that involves both small institutions such as family, friends, or a place like a farm or restaurant, *and* large-scale institutions such as the U.S. government and its policies. Policies and economic needs influence the types of jobs available to immigrant groups; consequently, different immigrant groups end up in an assortment of labor market niches.

Theories of social networks point to the social embeddedness of immigration—emphasizing the significant role played by family and community relations in the movement, settlement, and adaptation of immigrants. The social networks perspective has been deeply influential in the study of immigration, especially in the analysis of the development of migration streams. In *The Transnational Villagers* (2001), for example, Peggy Levitt describes how it is not simply a matter of coincidence that Dominican immigrants to the Boston area overwhelmingly originate from the village of Miraflores in the Dominican Republic. Rather, migration flows emerge through social networks that connect specific places of origin and destination.

Once immigrants are at their destination, social networks inform their efforts to survive in the receiving society, whether it is to find food, housing, or jobs. Social networks thus organize the occupational strategies of immigrants. From the social networks perspective, variations in the occupational strategies of immigrants emerge not simply because of differences in individual levels of human capital. Also relevant are variations in the character and qualities of the networks in which they are embedded. In *Modern Migrations*, Poros (2011) describes how social networks can be based on different types of social ties: those of kinship and village, and others based on shared connections to organizations, such as attendance at the same school or temple or employment in the same corporation. These differences, in turn, can result in divergent labor market outcomes among those with similar levels of human capital. She argues that social networks based on organizational ties may be especially valuable, enabling highly educated immigrants to more effectively harness the value of their educational credentials in the labor market.

One of the specific ways in which social networks shape immigrant occupational strategies is by channeling newly arrived immigrants into ethnic niches. That is, members of shared social networks refer each other to participation in the ethnic niche. In her ethnographic study of immigrant men from Yucatan, Mexico, in Dallas, Adler (2005) offers a vivid description of how social networks operate to channel the men into a niche in the city's restaurant sector:

> Men who already have jobs in Dallas restaurants, and have curried the favor and trust of chefs, become labor recruiters for those same chefs. Sometimes, either the chef or the veteran migrant will pay for the trip of the new migrant with the expectation that he will work in the restaurant to repay the debt. This happened with the case of Jose, a man who had migrated before but had returned to Kaal [pseudonym for town in Yucatan, Mexico]. Roberto, a man who had worked as a sous chef in a fine Italian restaurant, paid for Jose's trip so he could come to work in the restaurant. Jose had to work there for several months repaying his debt before he was able to switch jobs. This improved Roberto's relationship with the chef and, at the same time, improved his status in the migrant community. (236–7)

Social networks are then the core engine of ethnic niches, enabling their development and continuity over time. In essence, ethnic niches reflect the institutionalization of social networks. It seems natural that immigrant networks are a central force in the development of market niches for these groups, and they can often lead to opportunities for immigrants. As we will see through the examples in this chapter, however, the subsequent racialization of these sectors and the material implications of this racialization often create major challenges to the chances of success in these niches. The influence of immigrant networks can be contradictory, as some networks connect their members to favorable jobs that lead to greater opportunity, while others may limit the possibilities for their members by holding them in a certain level of work. Immigrant networks result in a variety of outcomes for their members not only because of the internal resources held by the network itself, but also because of the different circumstances that surround their formation.

Analysts have often emphasized the role of ethnic niches as adaptive formations that enable immigrants to cope with discrimination in the labor market by offering opportunities that they would not receive without connections. Indeed, in some cases it can be an effective path of upward mobility. Studies of immigrant labor movements have also noted how the network dynamics of niches can be advantageous in organizing workers to press for labor protections and rights (Milkman and Wong 2000; Milkman 2011). Hagan, Lowe, and Quigla's (2011) study of Mexican immigrants in the construction and building trades in North Carolina highlights how initial employment in the ethnic niche can provide a stepping stone to better jobs. They found that upon first arriving in the United States, the immigrants used their social networks to obtain work that would give them good opportunities for on-the-job learning, often through mentoring relationships with co-ethnics. After gaining skills, contacts, and U.S. experience in these trades, they engaged in a strategy of *brincando* (job hopping) to move into better jobs.

Based on her examination of West Indian immigrants in New York and London, Bashi (2007) reveals similar findings about the importance of social networks upon arrival. Bashi developed a network theory that outlines the specific roles of the network of actors involved in establishing the niches as immigrants settle into their new homes: the hubs and the spokes. The hubs are people who are settled immigrants already, but they use their experience and social capital to help new immigrants arrive and become established with a home and job in their new country. The spokes are those new immigrants who receive help and support from the hubs; they "achieve social and economic successes due in no small part to how their networks operate" (2007: 23). Just as Poros (2011) finds, the bonds formed in the network are crucial to its success. Bashi contends that the organization of these networks is "governed by the network's *culture of reciprocity*, a code that defines the resources to be exchanged among network members and the circumstances in which the exchanges should take place" (2007: 78). While hubs help spokes with a range of issues, when it comes to job opportunities, they tap into their own strong ties and consequently they are able to use their "employers in various schemes to ensure that their co-ethnics are hired" (2007: 179). Bashi finds that in this case, the West Indians do not rely on informal sector jobs or entrepreneurship like other groups, but rather they are able to "create *value for their ethnicity*" in the formal sector which affords them increased opportunities for mobility, as they are often hired as teachers and nurses (2007: 179).

Although the examples above show that social networks can provide beneficial opportunities for immigrants, there are important consequences to the operation of these networks in the formation of ethnic niches. While Bashi shows that the intricately connected hubs in the West Indian networks can lead to professional career paths, her framework and use of the phrase "value for their ethnicity" also demonstrates the complex interaction between race, ethnicity, and skill valuation in the job market. The process of occupational racialization occurs across a broad spectrum of jobs, as different ethnicities are valued for different roles. This process is complicated further by immigrant networks that lead people of similar backgrounds to continuously feed into a specific field. For the West Indian immigrants in New York and London, this stream into the service sector has been one of promise. The concentration of immigrants in one area of the market contributes to the reification of race and ethnicity, however: the identity can be seen as an immutable, biological characteristic that has implications for how people work. Race and ethnicity may replace skill as a qualifying attribute for a job. While there may be added emphasis in the informal sector jobs, the notion of race or ethnicity as a fixed trait that makes someone a good candidate for a specific role is present in the formal market as well. Many recent studies show that employers frequently "use race as a proxy for skill" (Maldonado 2006: 353) and employ terminology about "soft skills" (such as personality traits) as reasons for hiring people of specific ethnic and racial backgrounds (Zamudio and Lichter 2008). Additionally, Charles Tilly (1998) has described niche employment as a process of "opportunity hoarding" whereby valued resources are confined to members of an in-group. Ethnic niches may thus exclude already disadvantaged groups, thereby furthering their marginalization. In this way, they can enable and perpetuate the racial order themselves as well.

Ethnic niches and the social networks that undergird them are stratified formations that reflect broader social inequalities. Not only is race a fundamental element in hiring decisions, but other identities such as gender, social class, language ability, and immigrant status (undocumented, newly arrived) intersect to form a picture of the ideal candidate for the job, rather than just the knowledge and skill (human capital) a person has. For example, reflecting larger patterns in the economy, gender segregation marks ethnic niches, both within and across them. As we will see in the discussion of domestic service that follows later in this chapter, ethnic niches can take on masculinized and feminized meanings, which are in turn reflected in gendered wage disparities. In addition, ethnic niches carry the potential for exploitation of those within them. They encompass a wide range of industries and circumstances and they also vary quite a bit in what they offer to immigrants, in terms of pay, working conditions, and pathways of mobility. That is, some participants are better able than others to take advantage of the available resources of the niche. Among the multiple and intersecting axes of stratification within ethnic niches, immigrant status and legal status are often especially prominent. In other words, immigrants, especially those who are recently arrived and those who do not have legal status, tend to be particularly disadvantaged and occupy the lowest echelons of the ethnic niche.

For some, the racial stereotyping of certain jobs may help them to obtain employment, such as Latino/as looking for work in the hotel business (Zamudio and Lichter 2008). Yet even if the stereotypes help certain immigrants get hired, these same stereotypes are what keep them in low-paying, service-sector jobs. Although the Yucatan immigrant men in Dallas fuel the restaurant business in the city and almost every man who migrates from Kaal, Yucatan, follows their network into restaurant work, these men are most often found in the back of the restaurant (Adler 2005). Only a few immigrants have become waiters (which are typically white men in these restaurants), none are hosts, and none have become executive chefs, which demonstrates that these men are kept out of sight. Even as they become more settled and improve their English, the majority of the workers are in the low-paying jobs. The lack of mobility for the immigrant workers briefly discussed above is not only a product of the policies and entangled networks, but is also an effect of the process of occupational racialization.

The intersection of the axes of inequality influences the experience of immigrants in the U.S. job market. Axes such as gender, social class, and immigrant status matter, but when the process is seen through a race optic it is clear that immigrants who work in the United States are frequently sorted into jobs based on race. For immigrants, this process of occupational racialization is often disassociated from race, as other terms overshadow the racialized connotations. It is thus not always easy to see. In the current era, which many claim is "post-racial," it seems that the racialization of immigrants is overlooked because "immigration [status] does not trump race but, combined with the dominant ideology of a 'colorblind' society, manages to shroud it" (Hondagneu-Sotelo [2001] 2007: 14). Employers are able to speak about their immigrant employees in a way that is not explicitly racial, but more about "cultural differences" that immigrants bring to their new country (Maldonado 2006: 358).

In sum, social networks are a coping mechanism. Simultaneously, these networks may serve to enable and perpetuate the racial order by excluding already disadvantaged groups, thereby furthering their marginalization. By offering a steady stream of immigrants from the same area into jobs in certain niches, networks can also contribute to the association of certain characteristics with specific jobs: something that may lead to occupational racialization. But even as the social-networks perspective offers critical insights into ethnic niches, it also raises some questions. These include the issue of why ethnic clustering occurs in some occupational areas rather than others, and how the process of occupational racialization occurs and what its consequences are.

State Sponsorship and Empire

While some ethnic niches develop independently, without active government intervention, in many other cases they reflect state sponsorship. That is, in response to specific labor needs, the government actively recruits immigrant labor of particular origins for specific purposes. These recruitment programs, then, are embedded in larger projects of state-building and global power. In the contemporary era, the United States as the world's superpower has engaged in a variety of interventions—military, economic, and political—around the world. These interventions, part of efforts to maintain U.S. global supremacy in economic and political pursuits, often generate migration flows to the United States as migrants flee in response to the disruptions of U.S. intervention or cross borders to pursue perceived economic opportunity. These recruitment programs lay the groundwork for the development of social networks. Eventually the movement becomes self-sustaining and may continue even when the official program is terminated. Recruitment programs such as the Bracero Program (1942 to 1964), and nursing recruitment organized through colonial ties with the Philippines, illustrate how the U.S. government has been a driving force behind migration flows and how social networks take over in the aftermath of official programs. These two examples—one utilizing a reserve labor force across borders, and the other capitalizing on an imbalance of power created by colonialism—have resulted in trained reserves of labor that can be deployed as necessary due to such workers' subordinate position in the global racial order of white supremacy.

The Bracero Program

The experience of Mexican agricultural workers in the United States exemplifies the important interaction between social networks and state sponsorship. These workers began to come in large numbers as a consequence of immigration policy, but then continued to flow across the border into farms through networks. As discussed earlier (see Chapter Two), the United States has a long history of importing immigrant groups to serve as a labor force for the country's industries. Mexicans were legally brought into the United States for twenty-two years under the Bracero Program during labor shortages; when farmers saw that they could benefit from the low-wage workers (whose earnings were not regulated), the wages for American workers fell and the U.S. government ended the Bracero Program under pressure. Following the end of the guest worker policy, there were many Mexicans still working on U.S. farms. This continued despite the dismantling of the program. Though this government policy initiated many new immigrant streams into U.S. agriculture, the immigrants themselves sustained these streams. Bracero began "the institutionalization of migrant networks, which reduced the costs associated with migration for future migrants from Mexican communities" (Hagan 2004: 410). The flow of undocumented immigrants was constant even during Bracero, and consequently persisted after the program ended, so Mexicans continued to fill agricultural jobs because they had a pathway and were in demand (Martin 2002).

Although the Bracero Program ended in 1964, farmers' desire for cheap labor did not cease. This need has additionally shaped the experiences of immigrant workers throughout the twentieth century. Scholars are unable to discuss immigrants in farming without addressing the influence of the major food companies that have grown into huge conglomerates over the past sixty years. These companies thrive on cheap production of key crops such as corn and soybeans, and without a ready supply of immigrant laborers this system would collapse (Martin 1994). There continues to be a demand for Mexican laborers to come over the border because "immigrant workers continue to act as a subsidy" for the agriculture sector (Martin 1994: 57), and therefore they continue to come through the same migratory streams into the same jobs. The needs of the large companies have strongly influenced the government policies as well. Martin argues that the priorities of contemporary policies such as the Immigration Reform and Control Act of 1986 (IRCA) are not focused on "how to enhance the upward mobility of immigrant farm workers and their children" but, instead concentrate on "how U.S. agriculture should gain access to immigrant farm workers" (2002: 1124). With these goals in the background, it was inevitable that IRCA would not change the conditions of farm workers nor would it provide pathways for mobility; many of these Mexican immigrants therefore remain in low-wage, temporary, and unregulated jobs. This example shows how historical trends, big industry, and government policies intertwine to not only develop a labor market niche for Mexicans in agriculture, but also maintain the disadvantaged position of these Mexican agricultural workers.

While the looming policies and economic structure of agriculture in the United States and in Mexico have had a clear impact in developing the farming niche of Mexican immigrants in particular, the social networks of different immigrant groups interact with these broader forces in ways that can limit or extend the immigrants' opportunities. For Mexican agricultural workers, one significant element in the expansion of their networks that actually limits their ability to receive fair wages is farmers' use of labor contractors. The labor contractors serve as intermediaries between the workers and farmers (López 2007: 113). Usually the workers do not get in touch directly with a farmer; rather, someone in their social network connects them with an intermediary that they have come in contact with previously (López 2007: 113). The increased use of contractors by farmers puts workers at a disadvantage as the contractors typically exploit recent immigrants by giving them lower wages (López 2007; Martin 1994). The immigrant networks among farm workers link them to the contractors who help them to find employment, but it becomes a cycle for newly arrived immigrants to be taken advantage of by labor contractors, while those who are more settled eventually move from farm to farm looking for better conditions and year-long work without experiencing much job mobility (López 2007). And though many studies now confirm that new immigrants do not negatively affect Americans' jobs and wages, research shows "that the increased immigration of less skilled workers in recent years directly affects the labor market opportunities of immigrants themselves, especially earlier cohorts of less skilled immigrants" (Hagan 2004: 419). These immigrant networks (which have developed, in part, as a result of state sponsorship) that are typically characterized as support systems of people who help others to find work, in fact simultaneously contribute to a cycle that keeps the Mexican immigrants in the field with poor conditions and low earnings.

The U.S. government's Bracero legislation created and reinforced racialized images of Mexican immigrants as manual laborers. From the outset of the program, Mexican contract workers became known as *braceros*, from the Spanish word *brazo*, meaning "those who work with their arms" (Camarillo 2007: 508). Moreover, by promoting guest worker programs as mutually beneficial for migrants from struggling developing countries as well as for the national development of the United States itself, the programs are framed as different from other forms of more forceful and exploitative labor recruitment, such as trafficking in slavery and indentured servitude. By opening the economy to workers from failed economies of other "inferior" nations, the United States preserves its hierarchal position as a global superpower, both ideologically and economically. Such an idea of exceptionalism was present in the colonial conquest of the Philippines—an area that now provides one of the largest sources of foreign nurse migration to the United States.[3]

Filipinas in Nursing

The health care industry today is an increasingly important place of employment for immigrants. A variety of ethnic niches are evident in the industry. Among these is that of Filipina immigrants in nursing, who compose more than half of all foreign-born nurses. To explain the formation of this niche, we must turn to U.S. recruitment programs along with a larger history of late nineteenth and early twentieth-century U.S. colonialism in the Philippines. In her book *Empire of Care: Nursing and Migration in Filipino American History* (2003) Choy describes how ideologies of U.S. exceptionalism, with the mission of civilizing the world, served to shape its activities in the Philippines. These civilizing efforts included a particular emphasis on training in nursing, which would, as declared by Victor Heiser, the director of health in the Philippines, "transform them from the weak and feeble race we have found them into the strong, healthy and enduring people that they yet may become."[4] As the United States established specialized nursing schools that were based on U.S. models of nursing, it also established primary and secondary schools in English. With these efforts, then, the United States established the groundwork for creating a reserve army of skilled nursing labor.

Previously a Spanish colony, the Philippine islands were exposed to the practice of medicine, but the profession was reserved entirely for the male population. At most, women from the Philippines were only allowed to be midwives, and few were allowed to receive education to the same level as males. Women, particularly those of the elite classes, were encouraged to remain in the domestic realm (Choy 2003). The American system of colonialism in the Philippines introduced gender roles in the professions different from those promoted during the prior Spanish colonial system. Nursing in the United States was gendered as a feminized profession, and considered an extension of household activities related to care work. The conflation of nursing with care work essentialized the occupation as a female domain, and contributed to its devaluation in terms of low pay and benefits, setting the stage for occupational racialization as well (Tyner 1999).

In the context of colonialism, then, nursing became both a gendered and racialized niche. Since the goal of teaching the "backwards" Filipino proper hygiene and healthcare was central to the American mission, training in nursing was widespread despite resistance by Filipinos based on cultural ideals (Choy 2003). Speaking of the U.S. empire in the colonization of the Philippines, Espiritu (2003) notes:

> U.S. image-makers depicted Filipinos not only as incapable but also as unworthy of self-government. Both official and popular discourse racialized Filipinos as less than human, portraying them as savages, rapists, uncivilized beings, and even as dogs and monkeys. Viewing the annexation of the Philippines as a "divine mission," Theodore Roosevelt in 1901 characterized Filipinos as brute savages, uncivilized barbarians, and the heathen in the hands of satanic forces. (51)

The U.S. government used these racialized images of Filipinos to justify their colonial efforts to do political, economic, and social reorganization of the Philippines. It was the subsequent "Americanization" of the Filipino race through the establishment of American institutions that opened the gates of America when labor shortages called for recruitment of workers. Although women were encouraged to fill the nursing shortages in the United States, racialized imagery and stereotypes continued to influence the treatment of new Filipina nurses as they migrated across borders.

In the aftermath of World War Two, as the demand for health care workers grew with the introduction of the Medicare bill, the U.S. government saw the recruitment of foreign nurses from the Philippines as a solution to the shortage. From 1956 to 1969, over 11,000 Filipina nurses came to the United States, recruited by hospitals through the U.S. Exchange Visitor Program. Although the maximum stay of the visitor program was set at two years, many of the nurses overstayed their visas and were eventually able to obtain permanent resident status (Choy 2007: 562). Many Filipina nurses have entered the U.S. labor market through the occupational preference (H-1 visa) established in the 1965 Immigration Act. These preferences have enabled hospitals and health care companies to actively recruit nurses from abroad. The 1989 Nursing Relief Act facilitated these efforts by easing adjustment to permanent resident status for immigrant nurses and their families. Indeed, a large transnational industry has developed around the recruitment of health care workers, from the Philippines as well as other countries. By hiring foreign nurses, hospitals see reduced turnover due to contractual obligations with recruitment agencies, and also feel less pressure to raise salaries and increase benefits due to the perceived tractability of immigrant labor populations (Brush, Sochalski, and Berger 2004). Therefore, although the U.S. government established the initial pattern of Filipina nurse migration, hospitals using for-profit recruitment agencies have continued the pattern, and further established nursing as a gendered and racialized niche.

If the shortage of health care staff and the contributions of

Filipina nurses are acknowledged, it is also the case that they are the focus of nativist sentiment. In 2012, Filipina nurses won a legal case for a language discrimination case with a nearly $1 million settlement. The nurses, employees of a medical center in California, claimed that they were mocked for their accents and forbidden to use their native language at any time in the hospital. The language policy created a hostile work environment in which co-workers were urged to eavesdrop on each other and report any violations of the English-only policy (Do 2012). Under California law, employers can require workers to speak English if there is a business necessity.

As transnational bonds between the United States and the Philippines solidified both through colonial ties as well as more contemporary migration patterns, associations have formed to help protect against exploitation of Filipina nurses. These associations also serve the purpose of further establishing nursing as an ethnic niche for Filipinas. Organizations such as the Philippine Nurses Association of America (PNAA) offer mentoring programs and acculturation classes, as well as working to end unethical recruitment practices. Local chapters of the Philippine Nurses Association have also been active in attempting to build ties with American nurses and dismantle racialized stereotypes:

> Michigan PNA president Rose Tutay argued that Filipina nurses needed to move away from their stereotypic image as the "white-clad, brown-skinned, slit-eyed Oriental with long black hair who talks 'foreign,' who works quietly and [who] is ever willing to 'work a double' if the floor needs her" to a "better image of one who loves her profession, has leadership abilities, and can and does [do] her share for the improvement and betterment of patient care and better health care in this part of the world. (Brush 2010: 1578)

In addition to the risk of exploitation in the U.S. workplace, the movement of Filipina nurses abroad also provokes debates on the "brain drain" and consequences for public health in the Philippines. The push of a struggling economy and few job opportunities in the Philippines and the pull of a larger salary in the United States have maintained an unequal balance of power between the two nations, drawing skilled medical professionals out of the country that trained them.[5]

The examples of the Bracero program and Filipina nurse recruitment point to the formation of ethnic niches through both direct and indirect state sponsorship. While government legislation encouraging guest workers may be designed to be only a temporary fix for labor shortages, the very imposition of formal recruitment often results in continued migration, permanent stays, and in the case of Filipina nurse migration, entire new industries based on the continuation of such human movement. As the state, employers, private firms, and migrant social networks concentrate recruitment efforts from particular regions in specialized sectors of the labor market, racialized occupations become further entrenched. These state projects are embedded in white supremacy, establishing notions of essential difference and inferiority that further contribute to the marginalization of certain professions in terms of pay and benefits.

Emergence of Dual Labor Markets

The examination of state sponsorship programs highlights the dynamics of state intervention, which is often motivated by labor demands. From a differing perspective, dual labor market theories emphasize the role of economic structures in the formation of ethnic niches, especially those of labor. According to dual labor market theory, the economy of advanced industrial economies such as the United States is organized by a division of "primary" and "secondary" submarkets or segments (Doeringer and Piore 1971).[6] Workers in the primary sector are viewed by business owners as fixed labor capital—not easily replaced and thus worthy of investment. Primary sector occupations are "good jobs" with respect to wages, benefits, and working conditions. In contrast, the secondary labor market represents an underclass of occupations— jobs that are low-paid, unstable, and lacking in benefits. These low-end jobs have assumed particular prominence in the economy since the 1970s, as the U.S. manufacturing sector has declined. In the context of a global economic regime guided by neoliberal principles, the secondary labor market has expanded. Deregulation, the diminished strength of labor unions, and the rise of nonstandard work arrangements (such as subcontracting and on-call work) have all contributed to this trend (Harrison and Bluestone 1990; Kalleberg 2011).

As the secondary labor market has grown, so has the importance of immigrant labor within it. This has led Hudson (2007) to observe: "while migrant and noncitizen labor have always been a part of the American workforce, the new economy is now dependent on their labor in a way that was not true in the past" (290). As discussed in Chapter One, the late twentieth to early twenty-first century has seen growing rates of immigration into the United States. These "new" immigrants work in diverse sectors of the economy; however, there is a notable concentration in the secondary labor market. According to the Bureau of Labor Statistics, the proportion of the low-skill labor force that was foreign-born grew from 12 percent in 1980 to 50 percent in 2010. As Flippen (2012) notes, "these trends have been coterminous with a striking deterioration in the working conditions of the low-skill labor market, such as falling real wages and greater instability and informality in employment relations" (21).

The prominence of immigrant labor in the secondary sector has also been enhanced by the widespread departure from these jobs of those who were previously a core labor pool for them, including blacks. The Civil Rights Act of 1964 created alternative employment opportunities, especially in the public sector, for many black Americans. Also relevant were the attitudinal shifts among racial minorities that were fostered by the Civil Rights movement, including the expectation of a "decent job" whose conditions did not echo the racial servitude of the past. As these developments have occurred and heightened the significance of immigrant labor, there has also been a consolidation of the image and reputation of lower-tier secondary jobs as "immigrant jobs." They have come to be seen as inferior jobs that are not suitable for U.S.-born Americans. Moreover, although black Americans have distanced themselves from these types of jobs, because blacks historically filled them, the association of racial inferiority with those who are employed in this sector has persisted.

According to dual labor market theory, the use of immigrant labor reflects the imperatives of the segmented labor market, specifically the demand for workers who are willing to toil in secondary sector jobs. Immigrants from the global South form an ideal pool of labor for these jobs—expendable and easily replaced. They are seen as compliant and willing to accept poor working conditions, especially when disadvantaged by social class and legal status in the United States. In his analysis of the demand for immigrant workers in the United States, Massey (1999) also notes the significance of the transnational orientation of immigrants. In other words, immigrants evaluate the job with reference to the potential rewards that it will bring them in the community of origin:

> What employers need are workers who view bottom-level jobs simply as a means to the end of earning money and for whom employment is reduced solely to income, with no implications for status and prestige . . . Most migrants begin as target earners, seeking to earn money for a specific goal that will improve their status or well-being at home—building a house, paying for school, buying land, acquiring consumer goods . . . even though a migrant may realize that a foreign job is of low status abroad, he does not view himself as being a part of the receiving society. Rather, he sees himself as a member of his home community, within which foreign labor and hard-currency remittances carry considerable honor and prestige. (Massey 1999: 38)

For employers in the secondary labor market, there are also some particular advantages to the ethnic niche as a source of workers (Waldinger and Lichter 2003). Recruitment efforts are simplified as employers can ask employees to tap into their social networks in order to bring in additional workers as needed. The ethnic networks also foster worker discipline, as those recruited through them feel compelled to maintain a good reputation on the job, so as to not damage the opportunities of others in the community. For employers, then, the ethnic niche offers a "self-regulating and self-sustaining labor supply, that is, a labor supply that is self-recruiting, self-training and self-disciplining . . . The employer simply turns over the responsibilities of the labor process to the immigrant workforce, whose members organize and operate the work process through internal social networks and hierarchies" (Rodriguez 2004: 454).

Dual labor market theory argues that there are fundamental advantages to using immigrant labor for low-end jobs. As a result, policy interventions aimed at reducing immigrant workers in the secondary labor market are quite likely to fail. The various "get tough on illegals" measures that have been enacted in the contemporary era of enforcement are of questionable value. Instead of reducing the presence of undocumented immigrant workers in the economy, they simply drive that presence underground, masking it from the gaze of official authorities. For example, in an effort to avoid government sanctions for hiring undocumented workers, some employers have turned to subcontractors who hire the workers for them. The employers are then released from legal responsibility for their workers. In this way they avoid sanctions, but also continue to enjoy the advantages of using undocumented immigrant workers (Gentsch and Massey 2011; Massey and Bartley 2005). In her 1990s study of janitorial workers in Los Angeles, California, Cranford (2005) describes the growing use of subcontracted cleaning services by building managers. What resulted was a general deterioration in working conditions for janitorial workers, in a trend that negatively affected both documented and undocumented immigrants.

To summarize, dual labor market theories suggest that the formation of ethnic niches of labor is related to fundamental economic imperatives that also shape the racialization of the immigrants. As has been evident in the early twenty-first century, an ongoing demand for immigrant workers has had to contend with nativist movements to exclude immigrants. As we will explore in what follows, in the political contests that result, a notion of the "good immigrant worker" has been prominent.

The Politics of the "Good Immigrant Worker"

Skinning, gutting, and cutting up catfish is not easy or pleasant work. No one knows this better than Randy Rhodes, president of Harvest Select, which has a processing plant in impoverished Uniontown, Alabama. For years, Rhodes has had trouble finding Americans willing to grab a knife and stand 10 or more hours a day in a cold, wet room for minimum wage and skimpy benefits. Most of his employees are Guatemalan. Or they were, until Alabama enacted an immigration law in September that requires police to question people they suspect might be in the U.S. illegally and punish businesses that hire them. The law, known as HB56, is intended to scare off undocumented workers, and in that regard it's been a success. It's also driven away legal immigrants who feared being harassed. (Dwoskin 2011)

The opening decades of the twenty-first century saw a flurry of state bills across the United States, of proposed measures to "get tough on illegals." As highlighted by the Bloomberg BusinessWeek report cited above, businesses have struggled within this political context to legitimate their reliance on immigrant workers. As discussed in Chapter Two, their strategies have included the cultivation of rhetoric concerning the "good immigrant worker." Nested in American national traditions that valorize immigrants, the immigrant is portrayed here as a model worker—compliant, hardworking, and reliable. For businesses, highlighting the merits of immigrant workers justifies the hiring of them.

At first glance, the "good immigrant worker" may seem like a harmless or even benign concept that advantages the immigrant worker in terms of their value in the labor market. But there is also an underbelly to it. The "good immigrant worker" is another piece of the process of occupational racialization. Notions of the inherent suitability of certain immigrant groups for certain jobs can mask conditions of exploitation, making them seem natural and inevitable. In the context of the secondary sector, these ideas imply a natural and thus legitimate absence of opportunities for mobility into better jobs. Rather, these "good immigrant workers" are destined, by virtue of their inherent qualities, for employment that calls for tolerance of low wages and difficult working conditions.

Often underlying these ideas are racialized connotations that suggest immigrants who work in secondary sector jobs will never be "white," and therefore do not qualify for the same working conditions or opportunities. This understanding keeps the pendulum of immigrant imagery in motion, allowing for the "good immigrant worker" to rapidly morph into that of the "illegal alien" and "terrorist alien," as circumstances warrant. When there is worker unrest or a need to lay off workers, the image of the "bad immigrant" can be deployed to justify the dismissal and discipline of workers. In essence, the "good immigrant worker" legitimizes a singular notion of immigrants as useful workers who are expendable and are not owed anything beyond their minimal wages.

This notion of the "good immigrant worker," formed in relation to the needs of the dual labor market, plays an important role in the racialization of immigrant workers. The assertion of a fundamental immigrant difference offers a conceptual umbrella for the racialization of specific immigrant groups. In this era of color-blind racism, the commonplace use of subtle concepts such as the "good immigrant worker" serves to reinforce the racial order in the United States without being explicitly racist. In other words, as the concept of the "good immigrant worker" is applied to groups of particular origins, it also generates specific sets of racial meanings. In the contemporary U.S. economy, Latino/a workers, particularly of Mexican descent, compose an important part of the secondary labor market—in agriculture, food processing, as well as a range of low-wage service sector jobs. In this context, the "good immigrant worker" has been an important conceptual foil for the emergence of ideologies of Latino/a racial difference.

In her study of the fruit-picking industry in Washington state, Maldonado (2006) found employers praising the largely immigrant Latino/a workforce for their willingness, unlike natives, to work hard in these jobs; they were "good workers." This willingness was understood to stem from cultural inclinations— a "natural" Hispanic character. In accordance with color-blind racial ideology, notions of culture as innate condition were used to give form and meaning to that of a fundamental Latino/a distinction. We see these understandings in the words of Ross, one of Maldonado's interviewees. Ross was a white owner–operator of a midsized orchard:

> There are cultural differences . . . the Hispanic people, they tend to be a hard-working group of people. Their nature is to . . . do menial-type labour. They're . . . not ashamed to be labourers. There's no shame in that for them. Typically, [for] Caucasians, typical white society, that's a negative. If you're a ditch digger or a fruit picker, that's a low-end job and that's just . . . something that, the young folks aren't seeking to be, I guess. (2006: 355)

If the idea of the "good immigrant worker" has informed the production of ideas of inherent Latino/a difference, it has other racial consequences as well. Underlying the "good immigrant worker" is an implied conceptual dichotomy, between the immigrant and native worker. As immigrants are lauded for their eagerness to toil in tough jobs under difficult conditions, natives are concurrently condemned for not being willing to push up their sleeves and do the same work. Studies suggest that these accusations of native workers are especially likely to be directed toward blacks. For example, in their research on the hotel industry in Los Angeles, Zamudio and Lichter (2008) found employers comparing Latino/a immigrants to blacks in terms of their potential as employees. Latino/as, it was claimed, had desirable "soft skills," which were defined as the willingness to work hard without complaint and to concede to managerial authority without resentment. Black workers, in contrast, were described as uncooperative and uncommunicative and projecting a "bad attitude." These ideas, the authors argue, were used by employers to cast their discriminatory attitudes in color-blind terms. They conclude that "the bias inherent in screening for soft skills is in fact a bias in favor of workers who are perceived as more vulnerable and therefore more controllable. In this way, nativity is a proxy for degrees of controllability in workers" (Zamudio and Lichter 2008: 583).

Fueled by these dynamics of comparison, immigrant workers can become a particular target of resentment and hostility from natives. This is particularly so under a neoliberal global regime with the reduction of social safety nets. During this period when less-skilled workers find themselves squeezed by declining economic opportunities and jobs that do not allow one to live above the poverty line, immigrants can be a convenient scapegoat.

To summarize, from the perspective of dual labor market theory, the occupational strategies of immigrants reflect the opportunities and constraints of the segmented labor market. Secondary sector jobs need immigrant workers. The notion of the "good immigrant worker," embedded in the dynamics of the secondary sector, is a racializing construct. The employment advantage that it confers to immigrant workers is a double-edged sword, coupled as it is with defined limitations. The immigrant may be a good worker, but she is also an outsider who is not entitled to decent wages, benefits, or working conditions. Rather, she is destined by virtue of her natural qualities for employment that calls for tolerance of low wages and difficult working conditions. The idea of the "good immigrant worker" also serves to stigmatize blacks, condemning them because of their supposed unwillingness to work in bad jobs. These dynamics of comparison can work to damage relations between immigrants and black Americans, infusing them with a sense of competition and resentment. In this sense, the "good immigrant worker" is an idea that stabilizes white dominance and the U.S. racial order by weakening the potential for the growth of inter-minority alliances that could challenge it.

Paths of Mobility

As we have seen throughout this chapter, the various roles of social networks, state sponsorship programs, and the structure of the labor market interact with the racial organization of the United States to lead immigrants into trajectories that provide diverse opportunities. While these aspects of immigrant lives emphasize the structural forces at play, these are not the only elements that affect immigrants' settlement into the United States. In this next section, we further explore the immigrant experience in the U.S. job market by looking at paths that can often lead to social mobility, such as ethnic business and entrepreneurship, along with paths that may hinder the chances of mobility, such as the ethnic succession that occurs in certain professions.

The typical story of ethnic business mirrors the American Dream—if you work hard you can rise up in American society. Many classic stories emphasize the successful groups such as Cubans, Koreans, and Chinese who utilize co-ethnic ties to start businesses and turn a profit in a wage labor society that is plagued by an hourglass economy. In her book *The New Entrepreneurs: How Race, Class and Gender Shape American Enterprise*, Valdez (2011) argues that even these bootstrap stories that emphasize how particular groups have managed success have ignored Latino/as, blacks, and whites who have not achieved as much financial success in an entrepreneurial niche. Furthermore, these stories ignore the diverse class, gender, and racial dynamics embedded in a society that is structured by white supremacy, capitalism, and patriarchy. With the examples that follow we demonstrate how the intersection of race, gender, class, and immigrant status can condition the amount of social, market, and government capital available to entrepreneurs, which affects in various ways their ability to succeed in opportunities outside the dual labor market.

Ethnic Business

Entrepreneurship and small business are iconic features of American life. In the late twentieth and early twenty-first century, the celebration of entrepreneurship has been bolstered by the con-solidation of a neoliberal global regime that has encouraged the deregulation of markets and the slashing of government safety net programs (Gold 2010: 125). Immigrant entrepreneurs have been a particularly powerful focus for articulating these ideas. They con-stitute the heart of the American Dream, exemplifying the rugged individualist who through wits, determination, and industry, is able to carve out a slice of the American way of life.

In what follows we take a look at some of the complex realities behind immigrant entrepreneurship, especially that of small business. How has small-business entrepreneurship been part of the occupational strategies of immigrants? And how has it shaped the racialization of immigrants?

Available data do show that immigrants are more likely on average to be small-business owners than the general population. A 2012 Fiscal Policy Institute study[7] reports that the immigrant percentage of all small-business owners is 18 percent. This figure is higher than the immigrant portion of the overall population (13 percent) and the general labor force (16 percent). Immigrant business owners are evident in a range of professional and business service ventures, including fields such as information technology and accounting. Immigrant entrepreneurs have been especially evident in the leisure and hospitality industries, however, where they are 28 percent of all business owners. Immigrants are prominent as owners of hotels and motels, restaurants, taxi service firms, cleaning services, gas stations, and grocery stores. In terms of country of origin, Mexican immigrants constitute 12 percent of all immigrant small-business owners, followed by immigrants from India, Korea, Cuba, China, and Vietnam. Within the United States, immigrant small businesses are especially prominent in the metropolitan areas of Miami, Los Angeles, New York, and San Francisco.

Theories of Immigrant Small Business

The ethnic enclave perspective highlights the embeddedness of the ethnic business within an ethnic economy that brings co-ethnics together in complex chains of economic ties, from those of producers, suppliers, and retailers to workers. In essence, ethnic enclaves bring our attention to the ethnic embeddedness of immigrant small business. The ethnic economy itself is conceptualized as a segmented sector of the larger economy that is more or less autonomous from it. Some scholars emphasize the formation of ethnic enclaves or geographic concentrations in the development of ethnic economies. Thus in some businesses the primary consumer market involves co-ethnics while in others it is a wider customer base, outside the ethnic community, that is involved. In their analysis of the Cuban ethnic economy in Miami, Portes and Bach (1985) describe ethnic enclaves as "the spatial concentration of immigrants who organize a variety of enterprises to serve their own ethnic market and the general population" (203). Light and Gold (2000: 120) further note that "Ethnic-specific demand for native-language services and traditional products plays a key role in the development of ethnic economies because it shields the newly established proprietor from competition with more experienced and better-capitalized majority owned businesses." Whether ethnic enclaves are serving their own co-ethnics or a broader base, they are often able to leverage their specific knowledge and experience to help their business.

The ethnic economy has often been identified as critical to the occupational adaptation of immigrants. In essence, it provides immigrants with refuge from an otherwise hostile labor market. It may be an employment buffer, enabling immigrants without valuable employment credentials, English language skills, education, or legal status to gain an economic foothold. Other analysts, however, have tried to inject a note of caution, arguing that these notions are overly celebratory. What we may not know is how jobs within the ethnic economy can be "dead-end," and that exploitation among co-ethnics is not uncommon. Light and Gold (2000: 127) note: "Workers encounter difficulties in ethnic economies, including low wages, long hours and poor working conditions. Further, working in the ethnic economy yields few opportunities to learn English, which is normally required to move beyond bottom-rung jobs." The ethnic economy may provide social mobility for those who are able to rally their resources to be in the ownership positions; however, many obstacles remain in place for the co-ethnics who work for them.

Explaining Immigrant Entrepreneurship

Popular explanations for immigrant involvement in small business are often cultural in nature. That is, in ways that reify the boundaries of the group, they are seen as naturally inclined to small business, particularly even in a specific field. This propensity toward cultural explanation is highlighted by Nopper's (2010) study in which she interviewed representatives of banks and federal financial institutions to explore how they explained the concentration of Korean immigrants in business in the United States. The representatives spoke of the "entrepreneurial inclination" of Koreans and Asians more generally. We can see this in the following excerpt from an interview she conducted with the representative of a local MBDA (Minority Business Development Agency):

> for whatever reason they [Koreans] have that inclination. Not everybody has it. It's a mindset, an entrepreneurial mindset. Not having to rely on a paycheck every two weeks. Being able to get up in the morning and what you reap is what you sow, that kind of thing. That's an entrepreneurial mindset. And Koreans in general seem to have a lot more of that than most other cultures. (Nopper 2010: 75)

As Nopper (2010) argues, cultural explanations such as these suggest, if only indirectly, a certain cultural deficiency among other groups who do not respond to the opportunities and challenges of American life with the same entrepreneurial spirit. Such broad cultural explanations also have a tautological character—the fact that a certain group has high levels of small-business participation is taken as evidence of an entrepreneurial orientation. What is left uninvestigated are those many instances in which immigrants who do not have any prior background in business become entrepreneurs in the United States, often in fields that are completely new for them.

Given these issues, many social scientists have turned instead to understanding immigrant entrepreneurship as a reaction of labor market discrimination (Light 1984; Portes and Rumbaut 2006 [1996]. Entrepreneurship is then seen as an immigrant occupational strategy par excellence. It is a way in which immigrants cope with the disadvantages they face in the labor market because of discrimination, lack of English language skills, and thin knowledge of institutional practices of the dominant society. As Gold (2010: 13) notes, however, disadvantage alone is not enough for small business, which also requires resources, such as investment capital and access to cheap labor. Portes and Rumbaut, in their analysis of immigrant modes of incorporation, note how the character of the co-ethnic community can make a difference. Those that maintain norms of communal cooperation and money sharing, including rotating-credit and savings associations, are more likely to enter into self-employment.

While a variety of resource factors have been identified, a number of studies note the particular role played by highly educated immigrants in spurring ethnic economies. As we note in Chapter One, contemporary immigrants in the United States are bimodal in their class background. Among the highly educated immigrants, some move into professional jobs right after their arrival in the United States. But there are also those who suffer downward occupational mobility in the United States, where they are unable to find professional jobs due to discrimination, limited English skills, and unrecognized professional credentials. Accordingly, they enter self-employment because it provides them with better wages and working conditions than the alternative of entry-level positions in existing firms. As Steven Gold (2010) outlines, however, despite these negative conditions, highly educated immigrants bring an important mix of resources to entrepreneurial ventures: "Discrimination and out-group status notwithstanding, high levels of education helped immigrant entrepreneurs to master language skills, learn about new technologies and appreciate emerging markets. Finally, educational credentials yield prestige that can favorably impress community members, loan officers, fellow entrepreneurs, and others who can provide assistance" (2010: 131).

Model Minority Entrepreneurs: Indian Immigrant Scientists and Engineers

With the employment preference system of the 1965 Act, the 1990 Act, and the H-1B visa, many scientists and engineers have been entering the United States from India. They first come to the United States for higher study, often after earning undergraduate degrees in science and engineering from respected institutions in India such as IIT (Indian Institute of Technology). In many cases after earning their masters or doctorates at American universities, they obtain employment that then sponsors them (Kapur 2010; Varma 2011). Others have entered through the H-1B visa program as discussed in Chapter Two.

Indeed, as highlighted by the implementation of the H-1B visa program, Indian immigrant scientists and engineers have entered into a U.S. labor market that has relied on foreign labor, from India, China, and other countries. In 2003, 16 percent of scientists and engineers were foreign-born. Among foreign-born professionals, what has contributed to the particular edge of Indians is their English language ability and U.S. credentials. Even though Indian immigrant scientists and engineers do not encounter serious impediments to finding professional jobs, many report a glass ceiling, whereby they are excluded from managerial and administrative positions.

The relatively high rates of entrepreneurship among Indian scientists and engineers are often seen to be related to these experiences of discrimination. In other words, as is the case with other entrepreneurial immigrants, the strategy of business is a response related to discrimination. They have also brought a powerful set of class and ethnic resources to these ventures. This is reflected in the fact that their business ventures are often transnational, involving the global market and U.S.-India linkages. These developments have clearly been facilitated then by changes in India. Since 1991, the Indian government has implemented economic liberalization policies to facilitate foreign investments. Indian American entrepreneurs such as Sabeer Bhatia, co-founder of the email service Hotmail, have created global companies with linkages to India that take advantage of the availability of low-cost technical skills. Saxenian (2002) notes how they are creating transnational communities, building professional and social networks that span national boundaries and facilitate flows of capital, skill, and technology. The government of India has also been devising policies to attract Indians back to their home country. Since the 1980s as well, Indian immigrants have developed professional associations devoted to supporting business development. These include Silicon Valley Indian Professionals Association and the Indus Entrepreneur (TiE). Saxenian (2002), describing the formation of such organizations among both Chinese and Indian immigrants, notes how they "simultaneously create ethnic identities within the region and facilitate the professional networking and information exchange that aid success in the highly mobile Silicon Valley" (26). She interviewed Mohan Trika, a CEO of an internal Xerox spin-off called inXight:

> Organizations like TiE create self-confidence in the community. This confidence is very important . . . It provides a safety net around you, the feeling that you can approach somebody to get some help. It's all about managing risk. Your ability to manage risk is improved by these networks. If there are no role models, confidence builders to look at, then the chances of taking risk are not there. (2002: 27)

Yet other professionals have found success in a very different path. In her study of the South Asian franchise niche in Dunkin' Donuts, Padma Rangaswamy (2007) notes the important role played by a pioneering group of highly educated South Indians in developing this niche. Dunkin' Donuts is the largest coffee and baked goods chain in the world. At the national level, an estimated 50 percent of Dunkin' Donuts outlets are owned by South Asians, specifically Indians and Pakistanis. This clustering is particularly evident in the Midwest, especially in the Chicago area, where about 95 percent of these shops are owned by Indians and Pakistanis. Rangaswamy notes that the South Asian entry into the Dunkin' Donuts business began in the 1980s. It was led by men who found themselves in a position similar to that of South Asian men who ended up in Silicon Valley; they came to the United States for higher studies or under the preference quotas for professionals, but became discouraged after feeling discriminated against and so looked for business opportunities. As they entered the niche, they then sponsored relatives through family reunification—many of them less educated, whom they supported as workers, managers and business partners. The Dunkin' Donuts business niche became a major arena of economic incorporation for them.

The presence and success of entrepreneurial foreign-born scientists and engineers from India and China has excited nativism. But it is also the case that their role in the immigration regime and the larger racial order that underpins it has for the most part been to lend legitimacy to it. In the context of a neoliberal global regime, they have come to epitomize the values of immigration, of the continuing power of the American Dream. To be sure, they are also subject to nativist sentiment, blamed for outsourcing and the loss of American jobs. And this niche again reflects occupational racialization, though perhaps in a seemingly beneficial sense as notions of Indian immigrants as highly educated and upwardly mobile persist in popular discourse and perception.

Ethnic Business and Inter-Group Relations

As they organize the occupational strategies of immigrants, ethnic economies also shape the racial strategies of immigrants. Ethnic economies are complex arenas of interaction between groups. Perhaps the most attention has been given to conflict between immigrant business owners and blacks in impoverished urban areas. As Steven Gold (2010) describes in *The Store in the Hood*, there is a long history of immigrant store owners being targeted by customers. Contrary to popular view, however, these have involved a variety of groups. In the early twentieth century, Jewish and Greek small-business owners were often targeted by native whites and other immigrants (2010: 54).

The Middleman Minority: Korean Immigrants in Small Business

The middleman minority concept brings our attention to the particular dynamics that can surround immigrant small business (Bonacich 1973; Bonacich and Modell 1981). Jews in medieval Europe and in pre-war Poland, Asian Indians in South and East Africa, and Chinese in various Southeast Asian countries have all been described as middleman minorities. In all of these cases, the group in question plays the role of go-between or intermediary, bridging the relationship between the dominant and minority groups. Among the specific ways in which they do so is by setting up stores in minority neighborhoods where they sell wholesale products that they have obtained from the businesses of the dominant group. In this way the middleman minority fulfills the interests of the dominant group. It harnesses the consumer minority market and also insulates the dominant group from direct contact with the minority group. Indeed, in times of political crisis the middleman minority can be a convenient scapegoat, blamed by both the majority and minority groups for inequalities and conflicts. Reflecting these circumstances, middleman minority groups tend to be tightly bounded and marked by a high degree of internal solidarity. With the case of Korean immigrant businesses we see how the middleman minority can fill these roles.

Accompanying this notion of the middleman minority is the process of occupational racialization. As discussed, occupational racialization serves as one of the main obstacles for economic and social mobility—presenting a significant barrier to transferable capital for particular ethnic groups. When employers allow racial stereotypes to color job candidate selection, ethnic niches form in the labor market. Though bifurcated labor market theory assumes that pre-migration educational and economic capital translate into respective low- and high-skilled labor market opportunities for particular immigrant groups (Hagan 2004), understanding the complexities of occupational racialization allows us to see where high skills or education may not translate into congruous high-skilled occupations. As immigrant status intersects with race, English language ability, class, and gender in the American labor market, certain forms of capital that were once valued in the sending country may lose their effectiveness and become overshadowed by the ingrained system produced by occupational racialization. Immigrant groups may eventually internalize the idea that economic mobility is not possible in certain sectors, and further institutionalize the ethnic niche by following other members of their community who have found occupational opportunities. Faced with structural barriers, immigrants find themselves taking occupational detours in jobs completely different from or not commensurate with their educational level or previous occupation (Halter 2007).

Since the 1965 Immigration Act, South Korea has been an important source country of immigration to the United States. A history of U.S. military and political presence in South Korea has been part of the context in which these immigration flows have developed. Especially in the 1970s and 1980s, high rates of unemployment for college graduates as well as difficult university admission drove out large waves of Korean immigrants, which included many highly educated professionals. Middle- and upper-class Korean adults felt emigrating to the United States would provide a better life for their families due to the economic and political instability in South Korea. Because of the lack of established ethnic communities, many of the prospective Korean visa applicants desired to receive their chance at the American Dream through the occupational route as opposed to that of family reunification (Portes and Rumbaut 2006 [1996]: 71). As a result, Korean immigrants often have high levels of education and training. After arriving in the United States, however, most were unable to find jobs that were commensurate with their skills and credentials, often unrecognized and devalued in the labor market. Because of phenotype, immigrant language barriers, and unfamiliarity with American customs, such capital does not readily transfer into high-skilled or professional occupation attainment.

Reflecting these conditions, research indicates that Koreans are consistently under-rewarded in the U.S. job market. By surveying Korean immigrants in Atlanta, Min (1984) found that a majority of the immigrants faced status inconsistency in America:

> Two of the major status dimensions (race, education, occupation, and income) are unbalanced. Status inconsistency occurs when high race or education is combined with low income or occupation (underreward) or when low race or education is combined with high occupation or income (overreward). (336)

Today, Korean immigrants are most visible in labor-intensive Korean-owned small businesses, such as grocery or liquor stores, retail stores selling manufactured goods from Asia, or businesses catering to dry cleaning, manicures, or shoe repair (Min 2007). As discussed above, most Korean immigrants do not immediately start out owning a small business; after arriving, many Korean immigrants fail to find jobs commensurate with their skills. In the first three years after moving to the United States, Min's survey indicates that Korean immigrants tend to occupy blue-collar positions in the primary labor market, and the accessible white-collar jobs tend to have lower status than the positions they occupied in South Korea (1984). The respondents in the 1984 study indicated their realizations that structural disadvantages associated with being foreign with limited English ability prevented them from achieving economic mobility in blue-collar jobs or positions in occupational fields commensurate with their level of education and training. To escape the discrimination and prejudice they frequently encountered from native employers and co-workers in blue-collar positions, Korean immigrants sought out the autonomy associated with owning a small business. Korean immigrants did not see small business management as any less strenuous than blue-collar work in nonbusiness sectors, but they saw the opportunity for status consistency with the prospect of economic mobility through independently owned Korean businesses.

Thus Korean immigrants turned to small business as an occupational strategy. The types of businesses included grocery, liquor, and produce retail; retail of Korean/Asian–imported manufactured goods; dry-cleaning service; garment manufacturing; and nail salons. In 2000, the self-employment rate among Korean immigrants was 23 percent (Min 2007: 239). This figure is actually viewed as an undercount because of the under-reporting among those who work in the family business. Some estimate that almost half of all Korean immigrant men and women are employed in family-run businesses. Indeed, family labor has been of great importance in these ventures, enabling them to run labor-intensive small businesses such as convenience stores and dry-cleaning services. But since the late 1990s there has been a decline in self-employment rates among Korean immigrants. In his more recent research on Korean immigrant experiences in the New York–New Jersey area, Min (2012) notes self-employment rates in 2005 to be 27.2 percent, below the 1990 figure of 33.5 percent. This decline has also been accompanied by a gradual shift in

Korean American businesses from the retail to the personal service sector, including nail-care salons and dry-cleaning shops. Min (2007) also notes that the 2000s were marked by the expansion of many Korean businesses previously classified as small retail businesses to supermarkets and medium-size produce stores. These changes suggest that Korean immigrants have gradually switched from labor-intensive small businesses to medium-size businesses involving managerial skills and professional knowledge.

While South Koreans have experienced significant mobility in unexpected occupations in the United States, they often arrived with significant resources. As noted, the wave of immigrants that came after 1965 were largely from middle-class backgrounds; having sold their businesses prior to coming to the United States, many had the proceeds available to invest. Along with financial resources, their ethnic resources, including having high levels of ethnic solidarity, have given Koreans access to co-ethnic sources of advice, loans, business services, and saleable goods. Some research highlights the significance of Korean immigrant churches as places for ethnic solidarity and community building. At the same time, while vertical integration and niche consolidation offer competitiveness, high rates of self-employment in similar lines of business brought fierce competition and saturated the market. Thus there was a decline in the Korean fruit and vegetable stand business in New York City in the 1990s.

As mentioned earlier, an important facet of the Korean business experience relates to Koreans' position as the "middleman minority." Korean immigrants in New York City moved into black neighborhoods for business ventures in the 1970s after Jews and other white business owners moved out, placing them in this in-between social location. Korean-owned grocery, greengrocery, and seafood retail stores, and gift shops selling Korean/Asian–imported manufactured goods were overrepresented in minority neighborhoods in the 1970s through early 1990s. Not only in New York City, but also in Los Angeles, Chicago, and other cities, Korean immigrant merchants played the role of middleman merchants in black neighborhoods, distributing corporation-made grocery, greengrocery, and liquor items to minority black customers (Min

1995, 2008). The widespread departure from city neighborhoods in the 1960s and 1970s of many businesses created a vacuum in these areas, which provided the circumstances for Korean immigrants to enter into grocery and liquor stores (Min 2007). Reflecting the poverty and segregation of these areas, like other ethnic merchants who have occupied these positions before them, Korean merchants in black neighborhoods encountered boycotts and other forms of rejection by black customers beginning in the 1980s and early 1990s (C. Kim 2000; Lee 2002; Min 1995, 2007). In 1991 there was widespread outrage among black Americans over the case of Latasha Harlins, a black teenager who was shot by a Korean merchant, Soon Ja Du, while struggling over an unpaid bottle of orange juice. The anger spilled into the 1992 Los Angeles riots, during which approximately 230 Korean-owned stores were destroyed. While Korean merchants in South Central Los Angeles experienced many cases of physical violence, those in black neighborhoods in New York City encountered six long-term boycotts and nine short-term boycotts (Min 1995, 2007: 76). Jamaica in Queens, Harlem in Manhattan, and Flatbush in Brooklyn were major black neighborhoods where long-term boycotts occurred frequently in the 1980s and early 1990s.

While the dramatic nature of the 1992 Los Angeles riots highlights the conflicts between Korean immigrants and black Americans, many analysts argue that an exclusive focus on them is deceptive and indeed contributes to the stabilizing of a racial order of white supremacy. Min (2007: 241) points out that although it has not received as much attention, Korean merchants have also had conflicts with white suppliers. Moreover, as Jennifer Lee argues, an exclusive focus on conflict ignores the generally banal and indeed civil interactions: "the overwhelming majority are characterized by civility, routine, and the simple philosophy of business as usual" (2002: 84). Lee argues that it is not the nature of interactions with specific Korean merchants that lead to animosity. Black resentment stems from the symbolic meanings of nonblack business in black neighborhoods—the larger issue of black control over black community. In this context, the exclusive focus on conflict serves to enhance intra-minority division, thereby reducing the potential for alliance that could challenge white supremacy. Furthermore, Koreans, and Asians more generally, are placed in a fluid, uncertain position in which they slip between "good" and "bad" immigrants in ways that preserve their marginality (Abelman and Lie 1995). Again we see the good immigrant counterposed to the violent, poverty-stricken black American who is victimizing them.

In addition to its influence on Korean–black relations the Korean immigrant small business niche has also shaped relations between Koreans and other immigrant groups, especially Latino/a immigrants. The Korean ethnic economy initially relied on family and co-ethnic labor to meet its labor needs, but over time it has actively sought labor from other groups. This transition reflects the declining rates of immigration from Korea coupled with growing costs of hiring Korean labor. In his study (1999) of Korean small-business owners and their employees in New York City, Dae Young Kim describes how Korean employers saw retention to be a major problem with Korean workers who, after acquiring the necessary skills, left to set up their own stores. The workers were able to use their experience to achieve some mobility, and in turn co-ethnics became potential competitors. This left job openings for other immigrant groups to fill; Min's 1990 survey in California and New York showed almost 50 percent of employees in Korean small businesses to be Latino/a immigrants, specifically Mexican and Ecuadorian. As we have described earlier in the case of secondary sector jobs, the Korean employers expressed a distinct preference for Latino/a immigrants over black workers. Kim argues that a secondary labor market has developed within the ethnic economy. These relationships have been a source of conflict when labor laws are violated, exciting protest. In 2012, for example, the largely Latino/a immigrant workers of several Korean-owned supermarkets in Brooklyn, New York, launched lawsuits and tried to unionize to protest low wages and poor conditions (Semple 2012).[8]

As an arena of race negotiation, in the context of employer-employee relationships, Korean–Latino/a relationships reinforce separation and distinction. However, they have also generated new arenas of progressive activism. In her book, *Legacies of Struggle*

(2007), Angie Chung describes the activities of two organizations led by 1.5 and second-generation Korean Americans – the Korean Immigrant Workers Advocates (KIWA) and the Korean Youth and Community Center (KYCC). Both were founded to provide services for Korean immigrants, but have also expanded their efforts to include Latino/a immigrant workers and their families. They have engaged in these efforts even though they have brought them into conflict with powerful Korean business interests. Since the late 1990s, Latino/a youth have been participated in KYCC's after school and youth leadership programs and Latino/a immigrants have participated in business development and employment.

Reflecting the dynamics of social networks and niche formation, once the pioneers went into small business, it paved the way for co-ethnics to go into it. While these businesses face their share of failures, the trend of Korean small business in the United States has been to provide social mobility. Second-generation Korean Americans, for example, are likely to move out of small business and instead take up jobs in the primary labor market. The middleman position of Korean immigrants within the U.S. racial hierarchy, along with their social class in their origin country and ethnic resources in the United States, have also given them more options than other immigrant groups. While it is sometimes a barrier for immigrants to be chaneled into certain occupations, the pattern of small business development among Koreans has given them a more positive reputation as entrepreneurs, as discussed earlier. Consequently, the development of small business combined with seemingly positive racial and cultural stereotypes is used as a stepping stone for Koreans in the United States. Despite these stories of mobility, there are other entrepreneurial groups who have had varying levels of success due to occupational racialization, barriers to ownership or leadership positions, and additional factors such as gender inequality.

Challenges to Mobility: Mexican Gardeners

Based on research in Los Angeles, Ramirez and Hondagneu-Sotelo (2009) analyze the development of gardening as an ethnic business among Mexican immigrant men. While Mexican immigrants do not typically come to the United States with the same educational, financial, and racial or ethnic resources that Korean immigrants do, segments of the population have still forged their own entrepreneurial paths. These businesses often involve informal agreements in which Mexican immigrant gardener-entrepreneurs contract to provide routine lawn care services to homeowners or building managers. The gardener-entrepreneurs then come and work on the property, perhaps on a weekly basis, bringing lawn equipment as well as other Mexican immigrant employees. While these jobs have showed promise for some, this particular niche is limited in scope as it is part of the secondary labor market. Not only that, but the legacy of the negative racial stereotypes that Mexican immigrants face in the United States gives rise to significant barriers.

For much of the twentieth century, gardening was a Japanese American occupational niche, especially in California. But by the late 1960s, as the children of Japanese American gardeners moved into white-collar jobs, a process of ethnic succession began to take shape. This was a time when the Mexican immigrant population was growing, as well as diversifying occupationally, moving from agriculture into manufacturing, services, and construction. A background in farming produced a general sense of familiarity and affinity with gardening work. In addition, the development of the niche for them was also informed by an expansion of market scope. As part of a larger social trend of the commodification of household maintenance tasks, lawn care that was previously performed by family members was now being contracted out for hire. As Ramirez and Hondagneu-Sotelo (2009) note, whereas the hiring of a gardener was previously a luxury for the rich, the entry of Mexican immigrants into the occupation has coincided with a certain democratization of its availability. Lawns as important displays of status are a piece of a general trend of the expansion of service consumption for tasks that were previously done as unpaid labor.

Ramirez and Hondagneu-Sotelo (2009) argue that the gardening niche has been an important focus of entrepreneurship for

Mexican immigrant men, offering them significant opportunities for mobility. The hierarchy of the occupation involves three layers. At the bottom are the *ayudantes* or helpers, who are waged employees of the independent gardener or owner of the business. Helpers are generally recruited by the independent gardener through his social networks and may consist of kin. Helpers may aspire to become self-employed, to follow in the footsteps of independent gardeners for whom they work. In a sense, the time as helper is an apprenticeship, a time to learn appropriate skills and perhaps even to develop a potential customer base. The movement up into self-employment is contingent, however, on the ability to amass enough money to purchase equipment and to develop an independent customer base. To become the independent gardener, several elements must be in place. The workers must have the financial resources, but also English language skills and citizenship. For those who are undocumented, opportunities are further constrained by how this hampers the ability to get work permits, insurance, and licenses to own and drive trucks. At the top of the hierarchy are the landscape contractors who are generally not involved in maintenance, but in specific improvement projects. Landscape contractors are required to have licenses, pay state licensing board exams, and pay fees and bonds. Thus it is not easy to seamlessly enter into the role that provides the most mobility for the gardeners.

The case study of the Mexican gardening small-business niche highlights the complexities of the mobility question. The niche is stratified with potential for exploitation. It is restricted as an opportunity mainly for men, and despite the value the wealthy families place on the appearance of their landscaping, it is a job that is not highly respected, as it is considered low-skilled service work in the secondary market. At the same time, there are opportunities for some mobility, especially for those who are documented. Also of note is how the conditions of informality and the constant inflow into the occupation limit the fees of the self-employed gardeners, who complain of constant underbidding. The growing influx of Salvadoran and Guatemalan immigrant men into this occupation has also enhanced competition, creating conditions for inter-ethnic competition. In contrast to the entre-preneurship of the Indian and Korean immigrants, in this case we see lowered expectations of mobility within the secondary labor market. Mexican immigrants face the burden of occupational racialization, as they are historically seen as laborers or "service" workers in the United States, and that, combined with immigration status, education levels, and a lack of financial resources, severely limits their social mobility.

This example highlights that mobility is possible, but con-strained by many factors, particularly in the secondary labor market where positions of ownership and leadership are more difficult to come by. In our final discussion of mobility, we take a closer look at the consequences that the intersection of race, gender, and immigration status have on occupational strategies in a deeply racialized labor market niche: care work.

The Case of Care Work: Where Gender and Race Intersect

While we have examined occupational racialization as it refers to the way in which certain job sectors and those who work in those sectors are assigned reified racial meanings, it is important to con-sider that these meanings are not only reflective of skin color, but also derive from intersections with gender and immigrant status. These identities have implications that are not separate from each other. They reflect the "simultaneity and reciprocity of race, gender, and class in patterns of social relations and in the lives of these individuals" (Kang 2003: 823). To deepen the discussion, we include immigrant status as another ingrained identity that is experienced concurrently as well. Through a brief examination of domestic service and care work, it becomes clear that race and ethnicity are inextricably linked with gender and immigrant status in the formation of a racialized domestic workforce, having sig-nificant consequences for the occupation and the people that work in it.

Historically, domestic work has been an undesirable job in the informal sector that has been filled by a series of disadvantaged women from different backgrounds and ethnicities. This sector reflects the "ethnic succession" of the field, which has been a cycle of substituting one racial-ethnic group for another over the past century (Waldinger 1999). Whether it is cleaning the home or looking after children or elderly in the home, domestic service or paid domestic work is an occupation that is about the upkeep of the home and the care of its members. As is true of other care work[9] occupations such as nursing or counseling, paid domestic work is inherently personalistic and idiosyncratic (Hondagneu-Sotelo 2001: 10). This is especially so as it takes place in the arena of the home, with its deeply held ideologies of love, intimacy, and privacy. As a result, domestic service has a quality of invisibility as an occupation—an understanding of it as not a "real" job (Romero 1992: 21–2). This view can also give the racial dynamics of the occupation a certain opaqueness, masking them in an aura of personalism, a technique often used in color-blind racism.

Ethnic Succession and the History of Domestic Service

The history of domestic service highlights processes of ethnic succession. The entry of particular groups of marginalized women has been followed by their exit and replacement by another. Today in the United States, paid domestic work is overwhelmingly the province of immigrant women and often of Latina immigrant women. But this has not always been the case. Throughout the nineteenth century, at a time when job options for women were limited, poor U.S.-born white women were often compelled to enter into domestic service. They tended to do so, however, as a temporary strategy until they married.

There were also many immigrant women in domestic service at this time. In the Northeast and Midwest regions of the United States, young European immigrant women of Irish, German, and Scandinavian descent constituted an important share of the paid domestic work force. Irish immigrant women, often a crucial economic support for their families in Ireland, were especially prominent in the Northeast. In New York City in 1855, Irish women accounted for 74 percent of all domestic servants.[10] The stereotypical figure of "Biddy" (nickname for Bridget) as the Irish maid emerged in popular U.S. culture to stigmatize the Irish, to highlight their innate inferiority in comparison to Anglo-Saxon Americans (Urban 2009). Indeed, in the virulent anti-Irish public campaigns of the time, Irish immigrant women were a favored target of ridicule and hostility. Thus a *New York Times* article of 1872 described the Irish domestic worker in the following unflattering terms: "impertinent, shiftless, untidy, and gad-about, a steady invader of your larder, and sometimes of your wardrobe. These be harsh words. We confidently put it to almost any American housewife if they are not true words. Indolence and insolences are the faults of the Irish" (cited in Branch and Wooten 2012: 176).

The nineteenth-century vilification of the Irish domestic worker as "crude" and "savage" was accompanied by the notion that it was the mission of middle-class Anglo American women to civilize these deficient young women through benevolent tutelage. According to Amy Kaplan (1998), the ideology of U.S. empire—of America's "manifest destiny"—generated a parallel one of "manifest domesticity" in the home: "the empire of the mother thus shares the logic of the American empire; both follow a double compulsion to conquer and domesticate the foreign, thus incorporating and controlling a threatening foreignness within the borders of the home and the nation" (582). The civilizing mission of the Anglo American housewife was also evident in the Southwest and Western regions of the United States, where Mexican and Native American women dominated the ranks of paid domestic workers (Hondagneu-Sotelo 2001: 15). Andrew Urban (2009) has argued that middle-class women often eagerly embraced their assigned role as saviors of the immigrant women who worked in their homes. It was for the housewife a means of highlighting the significance of the domestic sphere to which she was confined, as well as of enhancing the authority and power she wielded within it.

The numbers of Irish immigrant women in domestic service began to decline in the late nineteenth century. Unlike the intergenerational occupational continuity experienced by African

American and Mexican American women, the daughters and granddaughters of European immigrant women were unlikely to go into domestic service. Instead they found work in factories or in white-collar jobs as secretaries or teachers. These intergenerational occupational shifts occurred in concert with a larger social change—the racial assimilation of the Irish. As discussed in Chapter Two, the late nineteenth and early twentieth century saw the "consolidation of whiteness"—the strengthening of "white" as a coherent and unitary racial category in the United States. As public attention turned toward the questions of racial difference posed by those of Southern and Eastern European descent, the Irish, to use Noel Ignatiev's (1995) dramatic turn of phrase, "became white."[11] Concomitant with these processes of racial assimilation, Irish American women faced a wider array of occupational options than in the past, enabling them to move out of the undervalued realm of domestic service.

In the early twentieth century, the composition of the paid domestic work force began to change in a process of ethnic succession. With the Great Migration,[12] African American women, who already constituted the majority of domestic workers in the South, also came to dominate the domestic worker pool in other parts of the country. Racial discrimination barred them from other jobs, including those generated by the expanding manufacturing sector. And unlike for their counterparts of European origin, domestic service for African Americans did not serve as a stepping-stone or a bridge of mobility into other occupations, either for themselves or their daughters. In their analysis of this history, Branch and Wooten (2012) argue that the early to mid-twentieth-century entry of African American women into domestic service was tied to larger social developments in both the U.S. racial order and domestic service as an occupation. The notion of a fundamental black-white racial divide and the prominence of African American women in the stigmatized work of domestic service mutually reinforced each other. Domestic service came to seen as a "colored job," in a reflection of the "natural" order of a world in which black women were inherently suited to domestic service in the homes of white women (Glenn 1992: 14).

By the 1970s, the presence of African American women in domestic service had waned. Among the transformations wrought by the Civil Rights movement of the 1960s was an attitudinal shift among racial minorities. African American women were increasingly likely to reject domestic service, with its potent connotations of racial servitude. There were also more alternative employment opportunities, in clerical and sales jobs, and in the public service sector occupations that had been opened up to racial minorities by the Civil Rights Act of 1964. Furthermore, this was a time of expansion in the market for domestic workers as growing numbers of women, including mothers of young children or daughters responsible for aging relatives, entered the paid labor force. For increasingly time-squeezed families and overburdened women juggling multiple responsibilities at home and at work, hiring help at home became an increasingly attractive option. This is especially so as domestic service has become a key sector of employment for immigrant women, and especially immigrant women of color in the United States.

Care Work and Racial Formation in the Contemporary Era

Among the notable features of the late twentieth–early twenty-first century is the prominence and visibility of global care chains in which women in the global South are employed to take care of children or the elderly in the global North, thus enabling women in the global North to pursue careers outside of the domestic realm. Care that once took place in personal homes is also increasingly taking place in daycares and nursing homes, assisted living facilities, and so on. This movement of immigrants into paid caregiver positions has many implications for childcare and eldercare both in the United States and in the immigrants' countries of origin (Ehrenreich and Hochschild 2002). Immigrant women who are themselves mothers take on paid caregiving jobs in order to ensure the economic well-being of their children. In doing so they may become separated across national borders from their children who are either left behind in the country of origin or sent back to the home country of their parents. What results is transnational parenting, which Dreby (2010) has described as "arrangements in which childrearing activities belonging to the realm of the production and reproduction of the family are scattered across national borders" (5). And as life expectancy increases in the immigrants' sending countries at a rate outpacing aging policy and program developments, these immigrants must negotiate care arrangements for their aging relatives from afar.

Studies have documented the tremendous human costs of the global care chain, deeply felt by those who are on its lower rungs (Dreby 2010; Parreñas 2005; Hochschild 2000). The separation across borders of mothers and children is at odds with widely held ideals and expectations of these relationships. These situations violate expectations of daily, face-to-face parenting in which mothers are constantly available to their children to meet their needs. The results are often difficult relationships filled with anger, guilt, and resentment. As they grow older, children may come to appreciate the economic contributions that their mothers have made to their lives through jobs abroad. Nonetheless, these relationships often continue to be emotionally fraught and in some cases result in estrangement between mothers and children.

For immigrants working as caregivers for the elderly while negotiating care for their aging relatives abroad, separation can be especially difficult. This struggle is particularly palpable when caregivers with strict values regarding respect for elders and filial piety must manage caregiving from abroad.[13] In his book, *Making Gray Gold: Narratives of Nursing Home Care* (1992), Diamond interviewed a nursing assistant who expressed her discontent with the commodification of care she witnessed in the United States:

> A nurse from a foreign country had just finished a contentious encounter with a resident, and frustration showed on her face while she tried to make sense of this most confusing social organization. "Oh, these people make me so mad," she said. "But there's one thing that makes me even madder—their families! If their families hadn't abandoned them, they wouldn't be here. In my country we don't even have nursing homes. Our families take care of their old." (70)

Within this passage, the sense of cultural differences in caretaking is suggested by the discourse of the foreign-born nursing assistant. By articulating a difference between what she views as the American treatment of elders versus treatment of elders in her own country, she essentializes herself as "naturally" suited to the occupation of caring. But just as immigrant caregivers blame American families for placing their relatives in paid care (in this instance, nursing home care), they themselves must arrange care for aging relatives in their absence.

The development of global care chains has been part of the growth and consolidation of domestic service as an occupation of immigrant women. In the United States, ethnic niches of domestic service and paid caregiving have emerged in different regional markets across the country. Immigrant women from Central and Latin America have predominated, but African, Asian, and Caribbean niches of domestic service have been evident as well. As is the case with the ethnic niches of other industries, those of domestic service are heterogeneous in many respects. There are often particular market and service specializations by ethnic group. For example, in the Boston area, Brazilian immigrants have a niche in housecleaning while immigrants from Haiti have clustered in elder home care services. There is also internal differentiation within these niches. In her 1990s qualitative study of Latina domestic workers in Los Angeles, California, Hondagneu-Sotelo (2001) describes a segmented occupation in which live-in housekeeping was the least preferred and thus at the bottom of the hierarchy. In contrast, weekly cleaning services were viewed more favorably and ranked highly within the occupation. Additionally, a 2012 study of foreign-born nannies, caregivers, and housecleaners entitled "Home Economics: The Invisible and Unregulated World of Domestic Work,"[14] illustrates how wages are segmented by race and immigrant status in the care work niche: "white domestic workers generally earned more than their black, Hispanic and Asian counterparts." Furthermore, "the researchers found that domestic workers who were illegal immigrants earned considerably less than those who were American-born or naturalized citizens" (as cited in Greenhouse 2012).[15]

Across these various differences, domestic service plays an important role, as it has in the past, in the racialization of immigrants. In the contemporary era, however, unlike the nineteenth century, employers are less likely to see themselves as part of a civilizing mission in relation to the immigrant women working in their homes. And due to norms of "color-blindness" today, they are not so likely to express explicitly racist attitudes, although it is acceptable to take note of and to discriminate on the basis of markers of foreignness such as language, dress, and food as well as essentialized ideas of cultural character (Hondagneu-Sotelo 2001; Moras 2010). Culture here is seen as an intrinsic, static quality that results in natural inclinations and proclivities. For example, among the stereotypes of Latina women are that they are maternal, warm, and patient. These inclinations are seen to distinguish them and make them eminently suited for domestic service, especially childcare. These seemingly benign stereotypes facilitate the exploitation of Latina women by promoting the idea that this work is not so difficult for them or not even work for them, given their natural tendencies. It is thus not deserving of the same level of compensation as other types of labor.

As described in Chapter Two, the politics of immigration in the United States today is dominated by concerns of enforcement, of the securing of national borders against the threats of the alien. As a care work occupation that is dominated by women, domestic service has always been a low-status job. These conditions of devaluation are enhanced in the current political environment, in which immigrants have been a focus of surveillance and suspicion. These circumstances highlight the foreignness of immigrants, providing support to the idea that they are outsiders who do not require the same kinds of privileges and resources as natives. Working conditions that are likely to be viewed as inadequate for the American worker become acceptable in the case of the immigrant worker who epitomizes difference from what is American. The notions of natural inclination toward domestic service and the "good immigrant worker" also support the idea that what these women do is not truly work for them—the work they do is not a real job. The fiction is one that facilitates exploitation, legitimizing low pay and poor working conditions. Furthermore, if these notions are specifically focused on Latina immigrant women, their racializing and gendered character is highlighted by the fact that their impacts extend beyond them to include Latinas more generally, including second and third generation Americans. That is, the imputation of natural, intrinsic difference is one that tends to gloss over other types of distinctions.

Organizing Immigrant Workers in Domestic Service

Maria Moctezuma's workday began at 6 a.m. and often ran until midnight when she was nanny, housekeeper, and cook for a family of four in Rancho Cucamonga. She hurried through her own meals in five minutes, she said, so she could get back to a long list of chores that included washing the family car, scrubbing the bathrooms, serving at late-night parties and caring for an infant and a toddler. She made $200 a week, below the minimum wage. "But I was desperate to work so I could feed my children," said the diminutive mother of four (McGreevy 2012, *Los Angeles Times*).[16]

Along with the growth of domestic service as an occupation, the late twentieth and early twenty-first century has also seen the development of a vigorous domestic workers' movement in the United States. Domestic workers are often seen as an especially difficult group to organize. For one thing, they often work alone, in households apart from other workers. These conditions of isolation are exacerbated in the case of live-in workers who may also have little contact with family and friends. And as we have discussed, the particular character and location of domestic service—in the private household—leads to the view that it is not real work and thus not a meaningful arena of collective labor action. These challenges are only compounded by the large presence of immigrants, including persons who are undocumented, in the occupation.

Despite these challenges, the domestic workers' movement has registered important victories. In 2008, Montgomery County, Maryland passed a historic Domestic Workers' Rights Bill after years of campaigning by domestic workers in collaboration with local community organizations. According to Cantor (2010): "this regulation oblige[s] employers to present a written contract to domestic workers and to offer them negotiation of the terms and conditions; as well as the specification of living accommodation standards. It also outlines a mechanism through which employees can file complaints in the event that employers do not comply with their obligations" (1061–2). Thus, domestic workers could establish set contracts outlining their schedules to avoid being overworked and exploited. Overcoming the isolation of domestic work by recruiting workers in public spaces where workers socialized and carried out activities, domestic workers organized with the assistance of policy advocates and attorneys of local organizations to push forward legislation in the local political sphere. Although many of the domestic workers involved were undocumented, they were able to frame the Bill by using human rights rhetoric as opposed to citizenship rights. They also appealed to sacred notions of the family and home and mutual employer-employee benefits to convince legislators to pass the bill. This landmark legislation led the way for further organizing initiatives by domestic workers around the country.

At the state level, in 2010, the Governor of New York David Patterson signed into law the Domestic Workers' Bill of Rights.[17] With this, New York required employers to guarantee overtime pay and rest days to domestic workers. The passage of the bill came after a six-year organizing campaign led by Domestic Workers United, an organization led by immigrant nannies, housekeepers, and elder caregivers that had previously worked in collaboration with the Montgomery movement. In 2012, the California state legislature passed a similar law. In this case, however, it was vetoed by Governor Jerry Brown, who argued that the insertion of workplace regulations into private homes was both difficult and problematic. The vetoed legislation called for protections similar to those that workers in other industries have enjoyed for years, including overtime pay and meal and rest breaks, as well as appropriate sleep accommodations for live-in workers and the ability to use employers' kitchens. Among the groups that opposed the legislation were staffing agencies, which also spoke of the problems of inserting workplace regulations into the home.

Despite the disappointment of the 2012 California Governor's veto as well as the issues of enforcement that have surrounded the New York bill, the passage of the legislation marks the important progress of the domestic workers' movement. A once invisible and undervalued labor market niche has come alive to challenge the low pay and few benefits associated with the occupation. The ability to successfully organize allows immigrant workers a chance at mobility out of domestic work, or at the very least, to refine the niche and demand fair pay and benefits for their work. The successes of the Montgomery movement illustrate that when the movement is framed as beneficial for both employers and employees and the role of quality care in the family and home are emphasized, care and caregivers become more valued and heard. Such movements are a step towards reducing the stigmatization of domestic work and making it an appealing, valued, and fair profession for those who decide to fill its ranks.

Conclusions: Occupational Strategies and Racial Formation

As we have seen through the course of this chapter, the various occupational strategies of immigrants are informed by a multitude of conditions. We see, for example, that ethnic niches are racial phenomena. Their emergence is intertwined with developments of the racial order. With the case of state sponsorship, we show that ethnic niches have emerged from projects of state power that are informed by racial ideologies. And as our discussion of labor niches in secondary sector markets reveals, the Civil Rights movement of the 1960s brought about changes in race relations that had important consequences for immigrant occupational paths.

Across the vast range of industries and jobs that they encompass, ethnic niches inform the racial meanings and images that come to surround immigrant groups and shape their ongoing racial location. We see that the process of occupational racialization is a dynamic and yet structuring process, one that is integral to the racial order. The various cases discussed demonstrate that the roles that immigrants fill in the U.S. occupational sphere allow some to achieve social mobility in the face of racial dynamics, while others are unable to overcome the particular barriers that they face. In the chapter that follows we explore the implications of these varied experiences for immigrant strategies of identity in the United States.

4

Immigrant Identities and Racial Hierarchies

The Irish who left behind a land of famine. The Germans who fled persecution. The Scandinavians who arrived eager to pioneer out west. The Polish. The Russians. The Italians. The Chinese. The Japanese. The West Indians. The huddled masses who came through Ellis Island on one coast and Angel Island on the other. All those folks, before they were "us," they were "them."

And when each new wave of immigrants arrived, they faced resistance from those who were already here. They faced hardship. They faced racism. They faced ridicule. But over time, as they went about their daily lives, as they earned a living, as they raised a family, as they built a community, as their kids went to school here, they did their part to build a nation.

President Barack Obama, January 29, 2013

In a 2013 speech,[1] President Obama speaks of a long line of immigrant groups who over time have become Americans, "one of us." He invokes a vision of America as a "nation of immigrants" that includes the idea of assimilation. The nationalist ideology of American exceptionalism has in fact often emphasized the assimilative powers of the country, conceptualized as the country's unique ability to take in diverse peoples and to absorb them. In this vision, even when immigrants face racism, over time the engine of assimilation can work its immense powers to make them into Americans and to ensure their acceptance into the national community. In its projection of a racially seamless outcome, this image of assimilation has meshed comfortably with late twentieth and early twenty-first-century visions of a "post-racial" America in which the country's racial divides, so prominent in the past, are no longer relevant.

In this chapter we explore the identity strategies of immigrants in the contemporary United States. That is, we look at how immigrants draw on available opportunities and resources to forge affiliation and community, constructing a sense of who they are and where they belong in the social and political landscape of the United States. Our analysis shows the identity strategies of immigrants to be varied, fluid, contingent, and powerfully anchored in racial structures, including those of a black–white divide. Immigrants do not just react to the racial order of the United States; they also shape it through their negotiations.

Theories of Assimilation

If the concept of assimilation has been intertwined with the nation-building project of the United States, it has also informed scholarship on immigration in the United States. Indeed, the assimilation paradigm has dominated U.S. scholarship on immigrant life during the twentieth century (Park and Burgess 1969). Born out of the influential Chicago School of Sociology in the 1930s, assimilation theory argued that immigrant groups were inevitably to move from attachment to "traditional" immigrant identities and culture toward integration into the "modern" mainstream of American life. Immigrants went through a "race-relations cycle" in which they assimilated over the course of several generations. Over time immigrants became "Americanized," shedding their loyalties and connections with the culture of origin and assimilating into the great melting pot of the United States. To be sure, assimilation was a gradual process, one that differed in its pace across groups. It did not happen overnight but typically took several generations to unfold. And due to better resources and opportunities, some groups were quicker to assimilate than others, as they made rapid gains in education and occupation and moved successfully into the middle class.

117

Scholars also noted that assimilation could involve processes of "ethnogenesis," in which immigrants and their descendants gradually merged into established and more inclusive groups, based upon newly realized affiliations such as those of nationality and religion (Glazer and Moynihan 1963; Greeley 1974; Herberg 1960). For example, immigrants who previously understood themselves in local, regional terms (members of their home village or province) began to see themselves in broader, national terms, such as Italian or Chinese. Or, as described by Herberg (1960) in *Protestant-Catholic-Jew: An Essay in American Religious Sociology*, immigrants could integrate into religious communities composed of persons of varied national origins. In fact, the final outcome or endpoint of assimilation was a matter of debate (Gordon 1964). Some noted "Anglo-conformity," or the complete melding of the immigrant into the dominant Anglo culture of the United States. In a more pluralistic outcome, immigrants were seen to preserve elements of their own culture even as they assimilated. But whether the outcome was "Anglo-conformity" or "cultural pluralism," there was agreement about the centrality of assimilation processes to the immigrant experience.

Based on research on the third- and fourth-generation descendants of European immigrants, scholars have affirmed that there is in fact a trajectory of diminishing ethnic distinction among European Americans over time. This is reflected in patterns of language use, residential concentration, and intermarriage (Alba 1990; Gans 1979; Waters 1990). The descendants of European immigrants were observed to practice "symbolic ethnicity." This is a voluntary type of ethnic attachment that is highly subjective and intermittent in character, centered on ethnic symbols, and entailing few if any sustained commitments. Indeed, those who practice symbolic ethnicity have a great deal of choice about their ethnic identifications. They can choose whether to claim a specific ancestry or instead identify simply as "American." They can also choose precisely which elements of their ancestry to emphasize and in what ways to express it:

An example of symbolic ethnicity is individuals who identify as Irish, for example, on occasions such as Saint Patrick's Day, on family holidays or for vacations. They do not usually belong to Irish American organizations, live in Irish neighborhoods, work in Irish jobs, or marry other Irish people. The symbolic meaning of being Irish American can be constructed by individuals from mass media images, family traditions, or other intermittent social activities. In other words, for later-generation White ethnics, ethnicity is not something that influences their lives unless they want it to. (Waters 1996: 200)

The 1980s saw mounting criticism of assimilation theory. There were growing doubts about the applicability of assimilation theories and the related concept of "symbolic ethnicity" to the largely non-European immigrants of the era after 1965. Responding to these criticisms, Alba and Nee (2003) offer what may be described as new assimilation theory. Assimilation, they emphasize, is best seen not as a particular outcome but as an ongoing and contingent process that shapes immigrants and the larger society in which they are situated. Assimilation is also best seen as an unintended consequence of immigrant efforts to improve their socioeconomic circumstances rather than a deliberate identity project of immigrants. Last but not least, Alba and Nee (2003) note that the assimilation framework may in fact not be so useful in the case of all immigrant groups, in particular not to those facing deeply entrenched barriers to their achievements and acceptance in U.S. society.

Another stream of revisionist assimilation theory has focused on the diversity of assimilation processes and outcomes. Developed in the 1990s by Alejandro Portes and his colleagues (Portes and Rumbaut 2001; Portes and Zhou 1993), segmented assimilation theory draws attention to the different paths of integration that can be taken by the second generation—the U.S.-born children of immigrants. The first path of "straight line" assimilation echoes that outlined by traditional assimilation theory, in which the descendants of immigrants gradually achieve upward socioeconomic mobility and enter the mainstream of the United States. The second path involves blocked socioeconomic mobility as the second generation confronts racial discrimination and limited economic opportunities. What results from the second path is a dysfunctional pattern of integration into disadvantaged urban minority cultures that are marked by an adversarial outlook of rejection and rebellion against mainstream norms and values, including that of achievement in school. The third path is of upward socioeconomic mobility concurrent with strong ethnic involvements. Here the second generation continues to identify with and be involved with the ethnic communities of their immigrant parents, even as they learn American ways. Portes and Rumbaut (2001: 52) argue that the type of selective acculturation that is part of the third path is especially important for groups facing discrimination because it ensures that children do not face the strains of adapting to the U.S. environment alone, without the support of their families and communities. It is, moreover, a strategy that ducks the pitfalls of the second path, in which immigrant children integrate into nihilistic minority youth cultures.

The Transnational Turn

Since the late twentieth century, the assimilation framework has also come under attack for its methodological nationalism: its conflation of "society" with the boundaries of the nation-state (Wimmer and Glick Schiller 2008). Scholars have emphasized the importance of understanding immigrant life in transnational terms, as embedded in ongoing movements, networks, and exchanges between the places of immigrant origin and destination (Levitt and Glick Schiller 2008). Transnational flows take a variety of forms, from economic remittances and political mobilizations to exchanges of ideas, values, and cultural practices. In a departure from the general assumptions of traditional assimilation theory, there has been an emphasis on the positive, supportive role that the transnational sphere can play in the incorporation of immigrant groups (Levitt 2001; Smith 2006). That is, rather than inhibiting assimilation, transnational ties can actually ease the adjustments of immigrants to U.S. society.

Transnationalism is clearly not a new phenomenon (Foner

2007). Not just today, but in the past as well, the lives of immigrants were embedded in ongoing connections between the societies of origin and destination. If transnational ties have always been part of the immigrant experience, they have arguably acquired greater significance in light of the acceleration of globalization. It is now easier than ever to be connected across borders due to technological developments in communication and transportation. Also relevant is the ascendancy in the late twentieth century of a neoliberal global regime that has pushed national governments toward policies that foster integration into global markets. International migrant remittances are critical sources of foreign exchange for many developing countries, often vastly exceeding official aid in their volume (Kapur and Mehta 2005). In the case of China, for example, the investments of overseas Chinese have been a vital source of foreign direct investment (FDI), fueling industrial developments in the country. Thus the transnational ties of migrants have attracted the attention of sending states, which have sought to actively nurture them through special diaspora programs and policies.

The growing prominence of transnational theories reflects a more general trend within the field of migration studies, of movement away from the paradigm of assimilation. This trend has been deeply informed by shifts in the U.S. immigration landscape. In the early twentieth century, when Robert Park and his colleagues at the University of Chicago wrote of assimilation theory, U.S. immigrants were largely of European origin. But since the late 1960s, with the influx of persons from Asia, Africa, and Latin America, this has no longer been the case. Also of note are the sharp challenges that have been evident in the post-civil rights era to assimilation as a normative process, especially when defined as cultural homogenization. There has been an emphasis on multiculturalism or the values of celebrating and even preserving (at least in certain respects) distinctive immigrant communities and cultures. This is suggested by the emergence in popular discourse of a salad bowl metaphor that evokes continued difference rather than melding, to replace that of America as a melting pot.

A Race Optic on Immigrant Identities

The assimilation framework conceptualizes race as an obstacle to integration that is also of variable significance. That is, for some immigrant groups, race is a prominent barrier to their successful assimilation, whereas for others it plays little or no role in their integration. A race optic, in contrast, views race as a central, organizing feature of the immigrant experience. From this perspective all immigrants, regardless of their specific characteristics and resources, face the ongoing task of negotiating the racial order and its divisions. Immigrant integration is thus best understood not in discrete but in relational terms, as marked by the efforts of immigrant groups to situate themselves in relation to others in the racial landscape. A race optic also suggests that these immigrant efforts have a fluid and differentiated quality, given the inherently unstable and intersectional qualities of race. That is, immigrant identity strategies are embedded in ongoing developments of race, as well as the complex intersections of race with other features of social inequality such as class and gender.

In what follows we use a race optic to explore the identity strategies of immigrants in the contemporary United States. As a point of departure, we organize our discussion around a set of concepts that have been important, albeit contested, points of reference in the current politics and culture of race in the United States. These are the pan-ethnic categories of "Latino/a," "Asian American," and "black." We explore these categories as social and political sites of immigrant racial formations. In their seminal work, Omi and Winant (1994) define racial formation as "the sociohistorical process by which ethnoracial categories are created, inhabited, transformed, and destroyed" (9).

Latino/as: Challenging the Racial Dichotomy

The terms "Hispanic" and "Latino/a" refer to those in the United States of Spanish-speaking origin or ancestry, or to those with origins in the countries of Latin America. These terms are often used interchangeably although there is difference in their

Table 4.0: How Hispanics Fare in the U.S.: Income, Education, and Citizenship 2010

	% of Hispanic Immigrants	Median Household Income	Bachelor's Degree or More*	Holding U.S. Citizenship**
Mexicans	64.9	$38,700	9%	73%
Puerto Ricans	9.2	$36,000	16%	99%
Cubans	3.7	$40,000	24%	74%
Salvadorans	3.6	$43,000	7%	55%
Dominicans	3	$34,000	15%	70%
Guatemalans	2.2	$39,000	8%	49%
Columbians	1.9	$49,500	32%	66%
Hondurans	1.4	$38,000	10%	47%
Ecuadorians	1.3	$50,000	18%	60%
Peruvians	1.2	$48,000	30%	62%
All Hispanics		$40,000	13%	74%

*Age 25 and older **Citizens by birth or naturalization

Source: Compiled from data in Motel and Patten 2012.

precise meaning. In a definition that has been adopted by the U.S. census, "Hispanic" includes Spanish language speakers from Latin America. "Latino/a," however, refers more generally to anyone of Latin American origin or ancestry, including such groups as Brazilians who speak Portuguese. In our analysis we adopt "Hispanic" when referring to census data, but otherwise use the more inclusive designation of "Latino/a".

In 2010, Hispanics were 16.7 percent of the total U.S. population. As shown in Table 4.0, 74 percent of Hispanics were citizens of the United States through birth or naturalization. At almost 65 percent of the Hispanic population, Mexicans were by far the single largest national origin group. Besides geographic proximity to the United States, the significant presence of persons of Mexican origin reflects the long history of migration, including the active recruitment of low-wage Mexican labor by U.S. industries throughout the twentieth century.

For Puerto Ricans and Cubans—the second and third largest

Hispanic national origin groups—the history of settlement in the United States has been somewhat different from that of Mexicans. Puerto Rican migration is deeply tied to the 1898 colonization of Puerto Rico by the United States and its subsequent status as an unincorporated territory of the United States. The 1917 Jones-Shafroth Act extended United States citizenship to all Puerto Ricans. In the course of the twentieth century, Puerto Rican communities emerged in the Northeast United States, especially in New York City.

For Cubans, migration to the United States is often traced to the 1959 Cuban Revolution led by Fidel Castro. The ensuing exodus out of Cuba was defined by the United States as a flight of political refugees escaping a Communist regime. The initial waves of refugees out of Cuba after the revolution contained many elite members of Cuban society with high levels of education and occupational skills. Many settled in Miami and Tampa Bay in the state of Florida, where they established thriving ethnic enclaves. These enclaves have eased the adaptation of the later waves of Cuban refugees, such as those of the 1980 Mariel Boatlift, who were generally less advantaged in education and occupational skills in comparison to the first wave.

Along with specific histories of migration by national origin, the integration of immigrants from Latin America is also shaped by their racial categorization as "Latino/as" and "Hispanics" in the United States. Given that these labels tend not to be widely used within Latin America, they are often associated with an experience of racial disjuncture as immigrants find themselves racially identified by others in ways that clash with their own understandings of themselves. In terms of a changed racial context, it is also the case that racial identity in Latin America tends to be viewed in relatively fluid terms, understood to be shaped not only by skin color but also by social class and culture. "Black" and "white" are seen not as dichotomous categories but rather as marking a continuum of racial identity. In advancing this argument, we do not mean to minimize the enormous differences across Latin America with respect to national histories and ideologies of race. Our point is rather that the racial schemes of the region are broadly distinguished by their relative fluidity in comparison to that of the United States.

These regional traditions of race are among the common themes that inform the identities of Latino/as in the United States. There are many dynamics of differentiation. The racial identity strategies of Latino/as are enmeshed in the multiple dimensions of difference and inequality within the Latino/a population, of national origins as well as social class and skin color. As shown in Table 4.0, 9 percent of those of Mexican origin are college-educated; the comparable figures for Puerto Ricans and Cubans are 16 percent and 24 percent, respectively. Median household income is varied across national origin groups, ranging from $34,000 for Dominicans to $50,000 for Ecuadorians. These socioeconomic differences intersect with another feature of Latino/a diversity, one that cuts both along and across national lines: skin color. Reflecting differences of skin color, Latino/as can face a range of racial labels in the United States, including (but not limited to) the polarized ones of "white" and "black." These differences feed into unequal social and economic outcomes:

> significant inequalities exist between light and dark Latinos within the same ethnic group that cannot be explained by differences in human capital or resources. Lighter and more European-looking Latinos generally do better than their darker counterparts in earnings, educational attainment, occupational status, housing, self-esteem and mental health. (Roth 2012: 140)

The procedures of the U.S. census are suggestive of the multiplicity of racial identities within Latino/a populations. The 2010 Census form first asked people whether they were of Hispanic origin, and, if so, which national origin. In the next step respondents were asked to check one or more of the boxes assigned to the five race categories—white, black, American Indian, Asian, or Hawaiian/Pacific Islander. The form noted, "For this census, Hispanic origins are not races." Thus those who indicated that they were of Hispanic origin were also asked to indicate their "race" using a choice of labels that did not include "Hispanic." Of those who identified themselves as Hispanic or Latino/a in origin in the 2010 census, 36.7 percent rejected the available categories by checking "some other race," while 53 percent of Hispanics identified their race as white, 2.5 percent as black or African American, and 6 percent with the category of "two or more races" (Humes, Jones, and Ramirez 2011).

Even as it does not classify Hispanics as a racial group, the U.S. census does collect and report statistics for Hispanics separately. For example, data on whites is often organized into a subcategory of "non-Hispanic white" and separate analyses are offered for Hispanics, regardless of their reported race. Arguably, these practices have meant that Hispanics are effectively treated as a racial group, even if they are not defined as such. More generally, the procedures and activities of the U.S. census have clearly served to institutionalize "Hispanic" as a category of identity and difference in U.S. life.

Moving beyond the census, there is much evidence to indicate that the concept of Latino/a has been an important, albeit contested, anchor of racial formation in the United States. Notions of intrinsic difference and inferiority from whites are longstanding features of the stigmatization of Latino/a populations in the United States. This is highlighted by the Mexican American experience, which has been a central site of Latino/a racialization due to both the historical and numerical significance of persons of Mexican origin in the United States. In *Generations of Exclusion* (2009), Telles and Ortiz note that the disadvantaged socioeconomic status of Mexican Americans today is rooted in the history of their incorporation through conquest and colonization. The United States legitimized its imperialist projects on racial grounds, citing the racial inferiority of Mexicans. These notions of difference and inferiority have continued to shadow the Latino/a experience.

As discussed in Chapter Two, the late twentieth and early twenty-first century immigration regime is one in which the "illegal alien" has been a particular target of state discipline and militancy. Latino/as have been closely associated with the specter of the "illegal alien." Thus the racialized meanings of "Latino/a" have been intertwined with that of "illegal alien," including its connotations of criminality, inferiority, and a quality of intrinsic oppositional difference to what is truly American. In *Brokered Boundaries* (2010), Massey and Sanchez draw on interviews with 159 immigrants from Mexico, Central America, South America, and the Caribbean living in the Northeast United States to argue that the contemporary immigration regime has strengthened Latino/a boundaries. Reflecting deeply stigmatizing conditions, Latino/a immigrants who had spent more time in the United States and had more exposure to natives were likely to reject rather than embrace an American identity. In relation to assimilation theory, these findings are counter-intuitive, suggesting as they do a march away from integration into America rather than toward it:

> During a time of rising anti-immigrant sentiment, repressive immigration and border enforcement, and the public portrayal of Latino immigrants as criminals, invaders, and terrorists, intergroup boundaries brighten rather than blur, and crossing becomes more difficult. The more time immigrants spend in the United States, the more contact they have with Americans and American society, the more aware they become of the harsh realities of prejudice and discrimination, and the more they come to experience the rampant inequalities of the secondary labor market. Rather than ideologically assimilating, therefore, immigrants become progressively less likely to self-identify as American and reactively reject the label. (Massey and Sanchez 2010: 212)

A political discourse of nativist anxiety about the growing population of Latino/as in the United States has been evident since the late twentieth century. At its heart is the menacing image of a "Latino invasion"—a takeover of the United States by Latino/as. The perception of danger that underlies this image rests on racialized notions of Latino/as, specifically of their intrinsic difference and inferiority and their subsequent inability to successfully assimilate to America. The well-known conservative scholar Samuel Huntington is among those who have voiced the idea of a "Hispanic challenge" to America. Hispanics, he observes, are a fast-growing population due to high rates of immigration as well as fertility. These conditions threaten the national identity and unity of the United States, given fundamental differences between Hispanics and Americans:

In this new era, the single most immediate and most serious challenge to America's traditional identity comes from the immense and continuing immigration from Latin America, especially from Mexico, and the fertility rates of these immigrants compared to black and white American natives. . . . [Americans] have overlooked the unique characteristics and problems posed by contemporary Hispanic immigration. The extent and nature of this immigration differ fundamentally from those of previous immigration, and the assimilation successes of the past are unlikely to be duplicated with the contemporary flood of immigrants from Latin America. (2004)

Let us turn now to the question of how Latino/as have responded to such stigmas as we have described. One strategy has involved the cultivation of pan-Latino/a political community, with an emphasis on the need for Latino/as of different national origins to come together and work collectively to protect their interests. Advocates of Latinidad or pan-Latino/a community have drawn attention to what is shared by Latino/as, from histories of Spanish and U.S. colonialism in Latin America to experiences of racism in the United States (Mize and Delgado 2012). The forging of pan-Latino/a political groups has been especially evident at the national level. Since the 1970s, such national organizations as the Mexican American Legal Defense and Education Fund, the National Council of La Raza, and the Congressional Hispanic Caucus have grown in political visibility. In generating a pan-Latino/a agenda, these organizations have turned their attention to issues that unite Latino/a communities, such as that of immigration reform. In doing so they have actively shaped the meaning and significance of a Latino/a identity in the United States. Thus we see how immigrants themselves actively contribute to the reshaping of racial categories and push the black–white divide to expand.

Despite internal political efforts to mobilize Latino/as into one group, analysts have also noted national origins to be the primary reference point of personal identity among Latino/as (DeSipio 2006). Studies show Latino/as to diverge in the extent to which they are inclined to identify themselves as Hispanic or Latino/a (Golash-Boza 2006; O'Brien 2008; Feliciano, Lee and Robnett 2011). Those who are U.S.-born and raised, for example, are more inclined to embrace a pan-Latino/a identification, given their weaker attachments to national origin identities in comparison to immigrants. Also relevant are social class and skin color, which intersect to organize the terrain of available identity options for Latino/as. Latino/as who are of lighter skin color and privileged class status may have the option of claiming a white identity. But for darker-skinned Latinos, a claim to "whiteness" may not be a credible option. The assertion of a pan-Latino/a identity may be especially attractive under these conditions. That is, claims to a Latino/a identity may be a way to deflect being labeled as "black" and confronting the attendant stigmas of this label. In her study of Puerto Rican and Dominican immigrant identities, Wendy Roth (2012) describes dark-skinned Latino/as to be especially likely to perform their Latinidad by adopting the cultural codes and actions popularly associated with Latino/as. Such strategies of racial distancing have been a consistent theme in U.S. history. Reflecting the powerful and deeply entrenched character of the black–white divide, immigrants have often tried to differentiate from black Americans in order to achieve greater acceptance from whites and even an amalgamation into "whiteness" (Brodkin 1998; Warren and Twine 1997; Waters 1999).

The racial strategies of Latino/as, whether defined by an embracing of "whiteness" or distancing from "blackness," are also shaped by the multiplicity of ways in which Latino/a affiliation can be signaled to others in the United States. Besides skin color, Latino/a identity is intimated in the United States by a wide range of cues, from language, accent, and surname to such matters as hairstyle, dress, and music. Latino/as may engage in strategic display or non-display of these cues in an effort to influence how they are seen by others in particular contexts. O'Brien finds that "both Asian and Latino Americans may regard themselves primarily with ethnic identifiers at times, and at other times through more pan-ethnic racial lenses" (2008: 9). These efforts highlight an important general feature of immigrant identities—their situational quality. Thus a Latino/a identity may be actively invoked by an individual in one setting but lie dormant in another, where it is less pertinent. What results is a "layering" of identities: "An individual of Cuban ancestry may be a Latino vis-à-vis non-Spanish-speaking ethnic groups, a Cuban-American vis-à-vis other Spanish-speaking groups, a Marielito vis-à-vis other Cubans, and white vis-à-vis African Americans" (Nagel 1994: 155).

For Latino/as, unlike European ethnics, this layering of identities takes place in relation to a "Latino/a" label that is widely understood to demarcate racial boundaries of essential difference from whites. Given this racialized context, Latino/as experience the field of identity options differently from European ethnics who have the privileged option of practicing "symbolic ethnicity" (Alba 1990; Waters 1990). Roth (2012) observes that even those Latino/as who have adopted mainstream American norms will likely not be seen as fully or legitimately "American," given the racial meanings of a Latino/a identity:

> Because "Latino" is a racialized category, it can be more difficult for Latin American immigrants and their descendants to lose a Latino classification than for other immigrants to lose their ethnic labels. Even if they have adopted the cultural behavior of native-born groups, an indication of Latino origins often leads to a reclassification. In this way, even when Latinos are viewed as an ethnic group, they are "racialized ethnics," perpetually defined as foreigners even after many generations and full acculturation to American norms. (156)

To summarize, the racial strategies of Latino/as are fluid and variable, informed by the many intersecting axes of difference and inequality within the Latino/a population: those of national origins, social class, and perceived skin color. Across these complexities is the shared backdrop of a Latino/a affiliation and its emergent racial meanings and significance in the United States. Reflecting on these conditions, scholars have argued that Latino/as occupy an intermediary "middle" space within the U.S. racial order (Golash-Boza 2006; Itzigsohn 2004; O'Brien 2008). Thus the increasingly visible Latino/a presence challenges the dichotomy of black and white that has organized race in the United States. But analysts have been less certain about whether this challenge augurs a fundamental shift in the U.S. race divide (Feliciano, Lee, and Robnett 2011; Lee and Bean 2007).

In his analysis of the developing racial landscape of the United States, Bonilla-Silva (2004) has proposed the emergence in the United States of a triracial hierarchy that resembles the racial order of many Latin American and Caribbean nations. Reflecting variations of skin color, Latino/as incorporate into all three segments of the triracial hierarchy. At the top of the hierarchy are whites, followed by "honorary whites," and then "collective blacks." Of particular note is the "honorary white" stratum, which he describes as including "most light-skinned Latinos (e.g., most Cubans and segments of the Mexican and Puerto Rican communities), Japanese Americans, Korean Americans, Asian Indians, Chinese Americans, Filipinos, and most Middle Eastern Americans" (2004: 932–3). "Honorary whites" are given many but not all of the privileges of white racial status. Their partial incorporation into whiteness serves to legitimize white dominance by offering an illusion of the porousness of racial boundaries and the potential for minority groups to access white privilege.

In what follows we turn to the identity strategies of another important minority population in the contemporary U.S. landscape: Asian Americans. As in the Latino/a case, Asian Americans are also a pan-ethnic group that has been seen to occupy a "middle" location in the racial order of the United States, which both affirms and contests black–white racial boundaries. Despite these important similarities, there are also profound differences in the character of Latino/a and Asian American racial formations.

Asian Americans: "Forever Foreign" and "Model Minority"

The 2012 census reported 17.3 million persons of Asian descent in the United States, comprising 5.6 percent of the total population of the country. In the U.S. census, the term "Asian" is defined to include those having origins in any of the original peoples of the Far East, Southeast Asia, or the Indian subcontinent, including, for example, Cambodia, China, India, Japan, Korea, Malaysia, Pakistan, the Philippine Islands, Thailand, and Vietnam. Asian Americans collectively compare favorably to the general U.S. population on many socioeconomic measures.

Table 4.1: How Asian Americans Fare in the U.S.: Income, Education, and Citizenship, 2010

	% of Asian American Immigrants	Median Household Income	Bachelor's Degree or More*	Foreign-Born Citizens
Chinese	23.2	$65,050	51%	59%
Filipino	19.7	$75,000	47%	67%
Indian	18.4	$88,000	70%	50%
Vietnamese	10	$53,400	26%	76%
Korean	9.9	$50,000	53%	58%
Japanese	7.5	$65,390	46%	33%
All Asians		$66,000	49%	59%

*Age 25 and older

Source: Data compiled from Pew Research Center, "The Rise of Asian Americans," http://www.pewsocialtrends.org/files/2013/01/SDT_Rise_of_Asian_Americans.pdf

College degrees are held by 49 percent of Asian Americans, compared to 28 percent of the general U.S. population; median household income is also higher ($66,000 versus $49,800). These general figures, however, mask the considerable socioeconomic diversity that exists across Asian American groups. Table 4.1 offers information on the six largest Asian-origin groups. We see that 26 percent of Vietnamese Americans have a college degree, far lower than the comparable figure of 70 percent for Indian Americans. These vast differences in educational qualifications are also reflected in a wide gap in median household income, $53,400 versus $88,000 for Vietnamese and Indian Americans, respectively.

A brief review of the migration histories of the three largest groups—Chinese, Filipinos, and Asian Indians—highlights the diversity of Asian American experiences. The Chinese were the first Asian-origin group to migrate in significant numbers to the United States. In the mid-1800s thousands of Chinese, largely young men, came to work in the expanding western frontiers of the United States. The Chinese Exclusion Act of 1882 effectively halted Chinese immigration, which did not resume in significant numbers until the Immigration Act of 1965. Since that time, the United States has received Chinese from Hong Kong, Taiwan, and the People's Republic of China. Chinese immigration has included persons of varied socioeconomic backgrounds, from highly trained scientists with advanced degrees to those with limited formal education and occupational skills.

Another particular immigration history, that of movement from the Philippines, is deeply tied to U.S. colonialism. The early twentieth century saw a movement of Filipino/as to the United States, largely to California and Hawaii where they engaged in agricultural work. The flows declined with the passage of the Tydings-McDuffie Act, which reclassified the status of Filipino/as from that of U.S. nationals to aliens and simultaneously restricted their entry to fifty persons per year. During World War Two and its aftermath, immigration occurred through the marriages of Filipina women to U.S. military personnel stationed in the Philippines. At this time there was also a movement of Filipina nurses to the United States through the Exchange Visitors Program. In the late twentieth and early twenty-first century, the U.S. medical industry continued to recruit skilled workers and professionals from the Philippines. Like many other immigrant groups, Filipino/a Americans have also established themselves in the United States through family reunification.

Prior to the 1970s, Asian Indian immigration to the United States was quite limited.[2] But in the years following the 1965 Immigration Act, Asian Indians began moving to the United States, often under the Act's occupational preference quotas. The decades of the 1980s and 1990s saw a sharp increase in the Indian American population as immigrants from India began to enter under the family reunification clause of the 1965 Act. Also of significance was the Immigration Act of 1990, which allowed Indians to enter the United States under the H-1B visa program, designed to recruit high-skilled workers from abroad in order to meet labor shortages in U.S. industries.

By examining these particular national origins histories it becomes clear that the concept of "Asian American," like that of "Latino/a," encompasses a wide range of groups with varied experiences of migration and settlement in the United States. Indeed, the heterogeneity of the Asian American population is in some ways especially striking, given the absence of a widely shared language and common history of colonialism. Even so, we would argue that the concept of "Asian American" has been an important site of racial meanings and processes, albeit a fluid and deeply contested one, for Asian-origin populations in the United States. At the heart of Asian American racial formations is the western imperialist project of Orientalism. Orientalism, as described in the writings of Edward Said (1978), is the posing of a fundamental, insurmountable difference between Europe/the West and the Orient / the East. The West is defined by its modernity, dynamism, universalism, and ultimately, its superiority. These qualities come to light in relation to the East, which is defined by its innate and particular religious and cultural traditions; the Orient is exotic, strange and unchanging, fixed in time.

Orientalism has informed the racialized construction of Asians as outsiders, an indelibly foreign presence in the United States. Studies have documented the many ways in which Asian Americans, even those who are second-, third-, or fourth-generation Americans, find themselves being questioned about whether they are truly and legitimately "American" (Kibria 2002; Tuan 1998). These experiences of "de-Americanization" range from the relatively mundane one of being questioned about one's English language knowledge to the more serious charges of disloyalty to U.S. national security and interests. The mass incarceration of Japanese Americans by the United States during World War Two is a stark and tragic example of the singling out by the U.S. state of an Asian American group because of their presumed disloyalty. While Germans and Italians in the United States were also declared at this time to be "enemy aliens," it was only the Japanese who were targeted for placement in internment camps. Despite the lack of any concrete evidence, Japanese Americans were forced to leave behind their homes and businesses and live in the camps. Almost two-thirds of those detained were citizens of the United States and many had never been to Japan. And also among them were U.S. veterans of World War I (Takaki 1998). In 1988, Congress passed and President Ronald Reagan signed legislation that apologized for the Japanese American internment on behalf of the U.S. government and also paid reparations to those who had been interned and their heirs. The legislation said that the actions of the United States government had been based on "race prejudice, war hysteria, and a failure of political leadership."[3]

In the contemporary era, hostility toward Asian Americans as representatives of a foreign threat has often been tied to perceptions of Asia as a threat to the dominance of the United States in the global economy. In the 1980s, a time when fears of Japan as a rising economic superpower were widespread in the United States, the case of Vincent Chin came to epitomize the potential for violence faced by Asian Americans. Vincent Chin was a Chinese American and a U.S. citizen who had lived in the United States since the age of six. In 1982, he was beaten to death with a baseball bat by white autoworkers in Detroit. The workers were angry with the Japanese, blaming them for the demise of the U.S. car industry, and they saw Vincent Chin as a representative of the Japanese. In the aftermath of the attack, Asian American groups banded together to protest the extraordinarily light sentences (a fine of $1,780 each and probation) meted out to the perpetrators of the crime.

The theme of immigrants as a danger to America and its natives has been present throughout U.S. history. Contemporary depictions of an Asian American threat are notable for how they focus not on the inferiority of persons of Asian origin but rather on their ability to rival and outperform other Americans. Along with an assumption of "perpetual foreignness," Asian Americans have also been seen since the 1980s as "model minorities." They are often depicted in popular culture as math "whiz kids," spelling bee champs, and successful entrepreneurs. These stereotypes suggest that Asians are an exemplary minority, culturally programmed for success. Reflecting the stamp of Orientalism, their success is tied to certain innate cultural predispositions, including a strong work ethic and commitment to education.

What then does the model minority stereotype signal for the

racial incorporation of Asian Americans? An optimistic assessment is that it gestures toward successful assimilation; Asian Americans are mimicking the trajectory of gradual integration taken by European Americans in the past. Their experiences offer evidence that the American Dream is still alive and well for those who are willing to work for it. With their exemplary achievements, Asian Americans fulfill the litmus test of American exceptionalism, indicating their suitability for full citizenship in the United States. Those who take this position make note of the fact that Asian Americans not only fare well on statistical measures of socioeconomic achievement, but also show relatively high rates of intermarriage. Based on data on newlyweds, or those married in the year prior to the survey, a Pew Research Center (2012) report notes Asian Americans to be more likely than others to be intermarried. From 2008 to 2010, 28 percent of all Asian American newlyweds married someone of a different race, compared with 26 percent of Hispanics, 17 percent of blacks and 9 percent of whites.

Yet a close look at the model minority stereotype reveals its hidden layers—an underbelly that contributes to the marginalization of Asian Americans, whatever their economic successes in the United States. Claire Kim (1999) has observed that "scholars in Asian American Studies have generated powerful critiques of the model minority myth, pointing out that it exaggerates Asian American prosperity, homogenizes this extremely diverse population, and obscures discriminatory treatment against it" (118). Indeed, the notion of "model minority" evokes a set of static cultural traits that serve to decisively distinguish the minority group in question. Thus, as a model minority, Asian Americans are indisputably foreign, not just despite their successes, but indeed precisely because of them. It is not surprising that the model minority, the object of applause at one moment, can rapidly morph into an object of hostility as the threatening foreigner. Thus Gary Okihiro (1994) argues that the model minority stereotype does not, after all, represent a favorable departure from the nineteenth-century image of Asians as a "yellow peril." The "model minority" and "yellow peril" are actually continuous images, he argues, vitally connected to each other:

It seems to me that the yellow peril and the model minority are not poles, denoting opposite representations along a single line, but in fact form a circular relationship that moves in either direction. We might see them as engendered images: the yellow peril denoting a masculine threat of military and sexual conquest, and the model minority symbolizing a feminized position of passivity and malleability. Moving in one direction along the circle, the model minority mitigates the alleged danger of the yellow peril, whereas reversing direction, the model minority, if taken too far, becomes the yellow peril. (142)

The model minority stereotype is also linked to the construction of a distinction, in public culture and consciousness, between the good, deserving minority—the model minority—and the undeserving minority. In this way the model minority group serves as a racial buffer, giving legitimacy to racial inequalities. The fact that there are some minority groups who can make it in America, effectively pulling themselves up with their cultural bootstraps, suggests that claims of racial disadvantage are simply an excuse used by some groups to justify their own deficiencies. Also of note is how the logic of the model minority stereotype feeds into that of neoliberalism and the global decline of safety nets for the poor. Finally, as highlighted by the history of the 1992 Los Angeles Riots, in its pitting of "model" and "problem" minorities against each other, the stereotype contributes to anger and distrust between minority groups. This reduces minority solidarity, thereby weakening the potential for developing minority political alliances that could effectively challenge white dominance.

Whether it is the "model minority" or the "disloyal minority," the concept of "Asian American" has been surrounded by a complex mixture of meanings that are suggestive of simultaneous acceptance and exclusion. Like Latino/as, Asian Americans are also often seen as a "middle group" within the racial hierarchy, intermediaries in an order that is organized around white dominance and the subordination of blacks. Reflecting on these conditions, Kim (1999) puts forth a theory of "racial triangulation" that analyzes how racial minorities are subject to different and interlocking forms of racial oppression. She describes a field of racial positions that is defined by the axes of superior/inferior and insider/foreigner. Within this field, Asian Americans undergo "relative valorization" as cultural processes fabricate a popular understanding of them as superior to blacks in terms of such qualities as achievement ability. Concurrently, Asian Americans experience "civic ostracism" as they are seen as "immutably foreign and unassimilable with Whites in order to ostracize them from the body politic and civic membership" (Kim 1999: 107). The dynamics of white racial power thus operate through the production of difference among racial minorities who are consistently evaluated in ways that reinforce the black–white divide.

Let us turn next to "Asian American" as a site of racial negotiation for persons of Asian origin in the United States. Resembling Latino/a immigrants, the racial strategies of Asian Americans have included an emphasis on collective pan-Asian political mobilization. In *Asian American Panethnicity*, Yen Espiritu (1992) describes how in the 1960s young U.S.-born Asian American activists on college campuses, inspired by the civil rights struggles of the time, organized the Asian American movement. Among the legacies of the movement is the very term "Asian American." Instead of the hitherto prevalent imposed label of "Oriental," "Asian American" signaled a means of political empowerment, a self-conscious and positive assertion of identity. Like the other pan-ethnic collectivities promoted by the movements of the time (such as Native American or Latino/a), the Asian American concept eventually became an institutionalized dimension of the contemporary U.S. racial system, often functioning as a basis for monitoring antidiscrimination efforts. Since 1980, the U.S. census has provided aggregate data on those of API (Asian and Pacific Islander) origins. Asian American Studies programs and classes have assumed a role on college campuses. More generally pan-Asian organizations and groups, both at a national and local level, have become an important feature of the social and political landscape of the United States (Kibria 2002: 15).

Along with these pan-Asian American formations, however, the late twentieth and early twenty-first century has also seen the proliferation of political mobilizations based on other axes of identity, such as national origins, Asian regional origins (such as

South Asian or Southeast Asian), as well as religion. These developments have been encouraged by the growing size and diversity of the Asian American population since the 1980s, which have enhanced the potential for political organizing along a multiplicity of lines. The trend toward differentiation in political life is also informed by the character of anti-Asian racism in the United States. As highlighted by such notable episodes in U.S. history as the 1882 Chinese Exclusion Act and the World War Two Japanese American internment, it is often a particular subgroup of Asian Americans, whether based on national origins or religion, which has been the specific target of discrimination. To be sure, the actual impacts of such discrimination certainly extend well beyond the targeted population so as to include a wider swath of Asian Americans. Take for example the aftermath of 9/11, when the U.S. government instituted a War on Terror in which Muslim populations were particular targets of suspicion. Indian Sikhs as well as other South Asians and Middle Easterners who were not Muslim found themselves to be affected by these measures and the crescendo of public hostility and anger toward Muslims that surrounded them.

If such experiences of shared culpability strengthen the potential for political alliances that stretch across specific Asian-origin groups, they also offer fertile ground for the development of strategies of disidentification. That is, if discrimination and violence toward a particular Asian group may act as a spur to pan-Asian solidarity, it can also provoke distancing. During World War Two, at a time of soaring anti-Japanese sentiment, Chinese Americans displayed placards and wore buttons that declared "I am not Japanese" to protect themselves from anti-Japanese sentiment (Hayano 1981). And in the aftermath of 9/11, some Hindu Indian Americans made a special effort to differentiate themselves from Muslim South Asians (Kurien 2006). In short, the dynamics of hostility toward Asian Americans have been such as to both encourage and discourage pan-Asian political formations.

Asian Americans have responded to the dynamics of racial exclusion through the cultivation of communities of national origin and transnational ties, as have Latino/as. In *Home Bound:*

Filipino American Lives Across Cultures, Communities and Countries (2003) Yen Espiritu looks at how Filipino/a immigrants in California construct a sense of "home." She argues that the racialization of Filipino/as undergirds these constructions in critical ways. She writes: "As colonized and racially marked immigrants in the United States, Filipino/as have been distanced from the 'national' or 'America,' blocked from full political and economic participation, and alienated from cultural Americanness, which was founded on whiteness" (2003:13–14). As a reaction to this "enforced 'homelessness,'" Filipino/as who live in the United States create strong networks within their families and communities (2003:13–14).

Within this context, Espiritu (2003) describes how Filipino/a immigrant constructions of "home" have been intertwined with assertions of patriarchal control in the family. Ultimately, she finds that they claim through gender the power denied them by racism. Echoing a prevalent theme in the immigrant literature, she notes how women, and especially second-generation daughters, become symbolic sites for immigrant families in the struggle to preserve authentic ethnic culture and identity (Purkayastha 2005). The behavior of daughters, particularly with regard to sexuality, thus becomes subject to intense scrutiny and control. The daughters of Filipino/a immigrants are policed by family members and urged to remain pure and true to Filipino/a culture. These efforts are enhanced by the immigrants' urgent sense of the need for cultural survival, which itself is informed by the racial exclusions they face in U.S. society.

If the policing of girls and their sexuality is one cultural response to racism, another view is offered by Hung Cam Thai (2008) in his study of Vietnamese immigrant men in the United States. Thai describes the emergence of a vibrant transnational marriage field in which these men return to Vietnam to find women to marry and bring to the United States. Toiling in low-wage secondary sector jobs, they experience both class and racial discrimination. Finding themselves in a disadvantaged position in the U.S. marriage market, they turn to a transnational marriage market. In Vietnam, they are able to use their U.S. earnings to gain access to women of high status. These experiences highlight the potentially important role of the transnational sphere in the racial coping strategies of immigrants.

In the contemporary United States, "Asian American" is associated with both intrinsic foreignness as well as superior achievement. In responding to the complexities of this racial location, Asian Americans engage in a wide range of shifting racial identity strategies, from the development of pan-Asian American political formations to the cultivation of transnational networks and identities. In their development and character, these strategies reflect the tremendous diversity of Asian Americans, with respect to national origins, social class, as well as other conditions that shape their opportunities and resources.

Let us now turn to the racial identity strategies of African and Caribbean[4] immigrants to the United States. As we have seen, Latino/as and Asian Americans are often seen as intermediaries in a dichotomous black–white racial order. For African and Caribbean immigrants in the contemporary United States, however, the challenge has been to negotiate a racial order in which they are seen as black. Reflecting its continued stigmas, resistance to being integrated into a black identity in America is an especially notable feature of the racial identity strategies of these immigrants. As we will see, African and Caribbean immigrants are an extremely heterogeneous population, composed of persons of varied national origins, languages, religions, and social class. This diversity tends to be overlooked, however, in the context of a racial order in which the boundaries of black have been seen and treated in intractable terms.

Black Immigrants, Black Identities and Racial Stigma

For black immigrants, confronting the American black–white racial divide presents a variety of challenges. In this section we explore the race and identity strategies of African and Afro-Caribbean immigrants who identify as "black" on U.S. government surveys. Just as immigrants from various countries in Central and South America find themselves condensed into a classification of Hispanic or Latino/a, U.S. categorization conflates the majority of African and Caribbean immigrants into a category of "black." Our analysis explores the experiences of those immigrants who are not only defined by others but also self-identify as "black". Consigned to what is considered the most stigmatized position in the racial order, many of these new immigrants strategize to change the stereotypes associated with blackness, perhaps by distinguishing themselves from African Americans. And as we have described with respect to Asian immigrants, they often see transnational engagements as part of a strategic effort to confront racism and improve their lives in the United States.

There is a long history of movement from Africa and the Caribbean to the United States, involving both the forced migration of slaves as well as the voluntary flows of those recruited to fill particular labor needs in the U.S. economy. Since the passage of the Immigration and Nationality Act of 1965, immigration from these regions of the world has increased dramatically. Family reunification has played an important role in this growth, especially for the larger and more established Caribbean population in the United States. Studies show the majority of recent Caribbean immigrants to have gained entry based on family ties (Thomas 2012; Capps, McCabe and Fix 2011). Immigration from Africa, in particular, has occurred with the passage of the Refugee Act of 1980 and the establishment of the Diversity Visa Program in the Immigration Act of 1990. These varied means of entry are reflected in the diversity of backgrounds and circumstances among black immigrants. For example, given the high school education requirements for entry through the Diversity Visa Program, highly educated persons constitute an important segment of the African immigrant population. In contrast, refugees arriving from war-torn countries like Somalia tend to possess lower education levels. The situation of refugees, however, is also differentiated by eligibility for assistance and resettlement benefits from the state. As we will discuss later in this section, refugee status also affects identity formations, distinguishing black immigrants arriving in the United States as refugees from those coming through family and employment-based channels.

Table 4.2: How Black African Immigrants Fare in the U.S.: Median Annual Earnings and Education, selected data, 2007–2009

	% of Black African Immigrants*	Median Annual Earnings**	Bachelor's Degree***
Nigeria	19	$36,000	35%
Ethiopia	13	$24,000	18%
Ghana	10	$30,000	20%
Kenya	6	$28,000	26%
Somalia	6	$18,000	7%
Liberia	6	$25,000	18%
Sudan	3	$21,000	23%
Sierra Leone	3	$31,000	19%
Cameroon	3	$30,000	29%
Cape Verde	2	$25,000	7%
Eritrea	2	$25,000	18%
Senegal	1	$25,000	23%
Uganda	1	$34,000	28%
South Africa	1	$26,000	22%
Guinea	1	$20,000	18%
Zimbabwe	1	$30,000	26%
Tanzania	1	$30,000	27%
Egypt	1	$35,000	40%
Morocco	0	$20,000	27%
Other West Africa	5	$24,000	20%
Other East Africa	2	$24,000	17%
Other African Countries	12	$25,000	18%
All Black African Immigrants		$27,000	23%

Source: MPI analysis of 2008–2009 ACS, Black African immigrants are those African immigrants who identify themselves on government surveys as black.
**Source:* MPI analysis of 2005–2009 ACS (Table 8) Median Annual Earnings for US Civilian Workers Aged 16 and Over, Black African Immigrants, 2007.
***Source:* MPI analysis of 2005–2009 ACS (Table 5) Educational Attainment for Adults Aged 25 and Older, Black African Immigrants, 2007.

Sources: Capps, McCabe, and Fix 2011.

As seen in Table 4.2, immigrants from Nigeria, Ethiopia, and Ghana accounted for 42 percent of all African immigrants who identified themselves as black on the 2008–9 American Community Surveys. The broad distribution of other African countries reflects the different policy measures designed to attract diverse immigrants. Overall, the socioeconomic profile of black African immigrants shows high levels of education, with 23 percent possessing a bachelor's degree (Capps et al. 2011) compared with 18 percent of native-born adults. Masters, doctorates, or professional degrees are held by 15 percent of black African immigrants (Capps et al. 2011). Despite these high levels of education, in the United States many African immigrants work in mid to low-level jobs, often in the service sector (McCabe 2011). Healthcare support occupations are especially prominent, with almost 14 percent of African immigrant women working in them. Just over 12 percent of African immigrant men workers and 9 percent of African immigrant women workers reported employment in management, business, and finance professions.[5] All of this suggests that movement to the United States often brings downward occupational mobility for African immigrants who must cope with the particular racial stigmas of a black identity in the U.S. labor market.

This pattern of over-skilled African immigrants working in low-level jobs is evident when we look at the median annual earnings of black African immigrants in contrast with the figures for black Caribbean immigrants in Table 4.3. Although only 13 percent of black Caribbean immigrants earned a four-year bachelor's degree, their median annual earnings averaged higher at $30,000 than that of black African immigrants at $27,000. Thomas (2012: 14) speculates that a combination of higher levels of English proficiency among Caribbean than African blacks, black Africans' tendency to attain non-U.S. university degrees, a larger and more established population of Caribbean immigrants, and the higher average age of Caribbean immigrants than of African immigrants contribute to these differences.

While 74 percent of African-born immigrants identify themselves as black on American Community Surveys spanning 2008 to 2009, the Caribbean immigrant population is more racially diverse, with only 49 percent identifying as black (Thomas 2012). Whereas immigrants from particular Anglophone West Indian countries overwhelmingly identify as black, the small share of black-identified migrants from the Spanish-speaking Dominican

Table 4.3: How Black Caribbean Immigrants Fare in the U.S.: Median Annual Earnings, and Education, selected data, 2007–2009

	% of Black Caribbean Immigrants*	Median Annual Earnings**	Bachelor's Degree (4-Year College)***
Jamaica	36	$32,000	13%
Haiti	31	$25,000	12%
Trinidad & Tobago	11	$32,000	14%
Dominican Republic	6	$22,000	11%
Barbados	3	$36,000	14%
Cuba	2	$24,000	8%
Grenada	2	$33,000	12%
Other West Indian Countries	2	$35,000	15%
Bahamas	2	$30,000	19%
St. Lucia	1	$27,000	12%
Antigua-Barbuda	1	$35,000	15%
St. Vincent	1	$32,000	14%
Dominica	1	$30,000	14%
Other Caribbean Countries	1	$35,000	15%
St. Kitts-Nevis	1	$31,000	18%
All Black Caribbean Immigrants		$30,000	13%

*Source: MPI analysis of 2008–2009 ACS, pooled; black Caribbean immigrants are those who responded "black" either alone or in combination with any other race to the ACS race question in 2000, 2006, 2008, and 2009.
**Source: MPI analysis of 2005–2009 ACS (Table 7) Median Annual Earnings for U.S. Civilian Workers Ages 16 and Over, Black Caribbean Immigrants, 2005–2009
***Source: MPI analysis of 2005–2009 ACS, pooled (Table 4) Educational Attainment for Adults Aged 25 and Older, Black African Immigrants, 2005–2009

Sources: Thomas 2012.

Republic and Cuba indicates their overwhelming choice to classify as Hispanic rather than black; the tendency to identify as Hispanic and not black reflects the more fluid racial order of their countries of origin, as mentioned earlier in this chapter. Table 4.3 shows that immigrants from Jamaica, Haiti, and Trinidad and Tobago represent 78 percent of all Caribbean immigrants who identify as black either alone or in combination with any other race.

For black immigrants, societal imposition of a racial "master status" conditions ways they form identities upon arrival in the United States (Waters 1999). Indeed, among the major questions surrounding black immigration to the United States today is that of their relationship and integration with the black American community. According to prevailing U.S. racial schemes in which any amount of African ancestry (the "one-drop" rule) makes one black, African and Caribbean immigrants are often seen as black (Shaw-Taylor 2007; Davis 1991). Given the U.S. norms of hypodescent, the option of choosing not to be black is one that is not easily available to them (Waters 1999). For many African and Caribbean immigrants, other social factors such as class, clan, or religion supersede race as the major axis of social differentiation in the countries from which they migrated (Guenther, Pendaz and Makene 2011; Bashi 2007; Shaw–Taylor 2007; Waters 1999). Moving from black-majority societies, where opportunities were conditioned by a combination of factors, to the engrained racial order of the United States, calls for black immigrants to negotiate where they stand and how they wish to present their "ethnic selves" in an environment that immediately defines them based on their "blackness" (Vickerman 1999). To do this, African and Caribbean immigrants practice a variety of strategies such as distancing themselves from African Americans, elevating their transnational identity, and in some cases, uniting with African Americans over a shared sense of racial oppression. Which strategy immigrants choose depends on a variety of factors, including time spent in the United States, experiences of racism, the geopolitical position of the sending country, gender, and citizenship status. Therefore while black immigrant groups find themselves labeled as "black" in the United States, their relationships and identifications with African Americans are nuanced and typically evolve over time.

The history of relations between African Americans and black immigrants reveals both solidarity and conflict. The late nineteenth and early twentieth centuries saw a small but important migration of African and Caribbean scholars who played a role of leadership in the budding Pan-African social and political movements of the time, forging alliances between black immigrants and African Americans. In addition, during the early twentieth century, Caribbean immigrants migrated to the United States to pursue economic opportunities in urban areas, and small numbers of African immigrants migrated as well, often for educational opportunities sponsored by American churches and missions (Blyden 2012; Waters 1999). During this period, black immigrants and African Americans studied together at black colleges and they also collaborated in the black Nationalist movements of the 1920s. Jamaican-born Marcus Garvey's Universal Negro Improvement Association (UNIA) addressed issues of racism in the United States, as well as colonialism in Africa and the Caribbean, generating enduring political ties between the United States and these regions of the world (Blyden 2012).[6] Throughout the years leading up to the Civil Rights movement, movements of solidarity arose between African Americans and black immigrants as together they struggled with residential segregation and hostility from the white American population.

But as a plethora of contemporary research on black identities notes, with the dramatic increase of black immigrant populations in the years following the passage of the 1965 Hart-Celler Act, more signs of hostility became evident. Since 1965, greater numbers of non-English-speaking African and Caribbean migrants have arrived in the United States. As mentioned earlier, along with a growth in numbers, migration from Africa and the Caribbean became more diverse in a number of other respects as well. The family reunification provisions of the 1965 legislation enabled migrants, regardless of their education levels and occupational skills, to join their family members in the United States (Blyden 2012). There were also growing numbers of refugees from Africa who typically entered the United States with minimal levels of economic and social capital, even as they had access to government benefits that are generally unavailable to other categories of immigrants (Brown 2011).

The growth in size and diversity of the black immigrant population has contributed to the perception of difference and division
between black immigrants and African Americans (Blyden 2012:
168). There is evidence that black immigrants themselves may stra-
tegically emphasize separation in an effort to distance themselves
from the particular stigmas of a black identity in the United States.
As we have seen in the case of Europeans, Latino/as, and others,
black immigrants struggle to position themselves favorably in relation to the black–white racial dichotomy of the United States. In
asserting distinction from African Americans, black immigrants
may draw on perceived differences, based on stereotypes, between
themselves as immigrants and black Americans. Popular images
of black immigrants "stealing" jobs and opportunities come up
against images of African Americans as lazy and dependent on
welfare (Blyden 2012; Vickerman 1999; Waters 1999). As native
and foreign-born blacks manipulate these images when using
distancing tactics, discord intensifies between the groups. By articulating their culture as hardworking and different from African
Americans, black immigrants feed into the oppressive color-blind
rhetoric white Americans use to justify an unequal social structure
and give substance to the charges that white employers prefer to
hire black immigrants over black Americans (Waters 1999).

Therefore, among the many conditions that give significance
to the national-origins identities of African and Caribbean immigrants, one of the most important is their potentially strategic role
as a tool for mediating black stigma. In the labor market, there
may be perceived advantages to invoking an immigrant identity,
specifically that of the "good immigrant worker" as we have
described in Chapter Three. Similar to Asian Americans, then,
these strategies have given rise to the "model minority" myth
for certain black immigrant groups (Model 1991). Furthermore,
African and Caribbean immigrant parents may purposefully steer
their children away from integration into the black American community. Like the black Caribbean immigrant parents described
by Mary Waters in *Black Identities* (1999), African immigrant
parents may see these efforts as important to ensure the educational achievements and occupational mobility of their children.

As suggested by segmented assimilation theory, they may see their children to be at particular risk for absorption into nihilistic urban minority youth cultures if they do not enforce this separate identity.

Social distancing by black immigrants from African Americans is not an inevitable process, however, and it varies depending on situational context, generation, and class position, among other factors. A more nuanced understanding of black immigrants and black identities, one that challenges the notion of a unilinear and homogenous trajectory of distancing from black Americans is offered by Balogun (2011) in her research on second-generation middle-class Nigerians in San Francisco. Underscoring the fluid, multiple, and situational character of identity formation, Balogun (2011) describes her respondents as actively negotiating between a black racial identity, an ethnic Nigerian identity, and an American national one. As discussed earlier with regard to the contextual aspects of Latino/a immigrant identities, here too all were potentially relevant, and depending on the circumstances, one could be emphasized over another. Balogun (2011) also argues against the idea that black identity has unidimensional meanings of stigma and that it is only a source of disidentification for African immigrants. The second-generation Nigerians she interviewed identified with middle-class black Americans: "They embraced a black racial identity that is neither oppositional nor associated with a downward trajectory, supporting the 'minority cultures of mobility' thesis that minority middle classes share a culture of upward mobility" (437).

Similarly, geopolitical dynamics, time spent in the United States, and citizenship status also shape the dynamics of racial identity and distancing. Based on research on immigrants from Haiti—a Caribbean nation where African ancestry predominates—Alex Stepick (1989) has written of the complex shifts that may occur in the course of negotiations of the racial environment of the United States. He describes how in the late 1970s and early 1980s, Haitian refugees in South Florida would often adopt an explicitly black American identity in order to cover up their Haitian origins. This was for them a strategy for avoiding the considerable stigma that was attached to Haiti and its people at the time, linked to stereotypes of disease (especially HIV–AIDS) and poverty. Over time, however, this strategy dissipated as Haitian migration slowed and the community began to establish a social and political foothold in the United States. Indeed, the community began to position itself differently, with community leaders asserting distinction from black Americans. Fearful of the absorption of the younger generation of Haitian youth into oppositional urban minority youth culture, Haitian parents emphasized ties to the Haitian community in an attempt to shield them from it (Portes and Stepick 1993; Stepick et al. 2001).

In contrast, the history of United States–Liberia relations, including the granting of refugee status to Liberians, has generated a different set of identity dynamics among immigrants from this West African nation. In her fieldwork with Liberians in California, Hana Brown (2011) finds that Liberians use their refugee status to legitimize claims to social and legal rights in the United States, as well as to distance themselves from black Americans. A feeling of isolation from their home-country networks of family and friends, coupled with an understanding that the United States was complicit in the development of the civil strife that ravaged Liberia, drive these refugees to make claims on the government by defining themselves as "deserving" of welfare and settlement services.[7] After negative encounters with poor African Americans in their communities, coupled with a growing awareness of the disadvantages of being black in the U.S., Liberian refugees develop an account of themselves in which they emphasize the positive, caring nature of their relationship to the U.S. state. They define this relationship as a counterpoint to that of African Americans, who they describe as "selfish, exploitative of strangers, and lazy individuals" who are, ultimately, "failed citizens" (Brown 2011: 155–8).

For Liberians as for other refugee groups, the process of adaptation to the receiving society is shaped not only by the dynamics of state sponsorship, but also by those of community networks disrupted by political turmoil and conflict. Generally speaking, unlike refugees, immigrants who arrive in the United States through family reunification, employment opportunities, or other means can more effectively turn for support to established and intact transnational social networks. Under these conditions, they may turn to transnational practices as strategies to cope with racism and to guide their relations with African Americans (Bashi 2007; Rogers 2001; Arthur 2000). In his comparative analysis of West Indian immigrants and African Americans, anthropologist John Ogbu distinguishes between the situation of the former as an example of a voluntary minority and the latter as an example of an involuntary minority that arrived in the United States under duress. Among the particular resources of voluntary minorities is their ability to use the homeland as a frame of reference effectively (as cited in Waters 1999: 142). In other words, when facing discrimination in the United States, West Indians may refer to their higher status in the country of origin as a way to resist the degradations of racism. Similarly, among the African immigrants he surveyed, Arthur (2000: 127) found many who view themselves as "sojourners" or temporary residents; they are in the United States to achieve educational or economic opportunities that will eventually provide them with enough capital to establish businesses in their sending countries. This identity as sojourners allows African immigrants to focus on the relatively higher economic gains to be made in America versus the country of origin, resulting in a stance of relative acquiescence toward racial inequality in the United States, despite experiences of racism (Arthur 2000: 75). Reuel Rogers (2001) echoes these ideas in his discussion of the "myth of return": an identity practice that Afro-Caribbean immigrants use to help ignore or cope with experiences of racism. He states:

> Afro-Caribbean immigrants have an *exit* option for responding to American racism. If the immigrants find their mobility blocked by insuperable racial barriers, they will likely maintain their transnational attachments and keep the "myth of return" alive. In such instances the myth of return becomes an option for escape or exit, which coincidentally may dampen the immigrants' interest in political participation in general, or radical political action or systemic reform more specifically. Rather than make costly political demands for reform, the immigrants can simply exit the political system. (2001: 184)

These often unrealized dreams to return to the sending country can affect how black immigrants relate to the political environment of the United States, including their relations with African Americans. Some argue that the transnational identity option open to black immigrant groups has discouraged the formation of movements of solidarity between them and African Americans, movements that could combat the black–white racial order and its attendant inequalities.

For many African and Caribbean immigrants today, the society of origin remains a primary point of identity reference, one that also organizes community life. Social networks based on place of origin ties provide crucial economic, political, and psychological support in the process of adaptation to U.S. life (Arthur 2000). Analysts have noted that the maintenance by contemporary black immigrants of strong ethnic communities in the United States has protected them to some degree from the racism that is directed toward black Americans in the primary labor market (Bashi 2007). The protection from racism offered by ethnic networks and niches weakens, however, over time. Second-generation black immigrants tend to hold a frame of reference and occupational goals that are different from their parents. These changes highlight the potential for new identity formations and strategies for combatting racism among later-generation African and Caribbean immigrants (Bashi 2007).

Transnational identities and practices can also be shaped by gender, as Mary Johnson Osirim (2012) discovered in her interviews with African entrepreneurs and civic leaders in Philadelphia and Boston. Her study reveals both men and women to be engaged in transnational activities, such as sending remittances to families in the homeland. But she also found African immigrant women to be more likely than African immigrant men to participate in local civic and community organizations in the United States. Some of these women felt that movement to the United States had freed them from their "traditional" lives, resulting in greater empowerment. Osirim writes, "As women of color, they [African immigrant women] face many challenges in the Greater Philadelphia and Boston areas, but most of them argue that life has been better for them in the United States" (2012: 227). Armed with a new-found sense of confidence, some of the women entered into small business. Others took on roles of leadership in communities and schools, bringing ideologies of Pan-Africanism into local struggles and alliances with African American residents and infusing them with new meanings and significance (Osirim 2012).

Osirim describes the Pan-Africanism emerging in the communities she studied as different from its earlier threads in the United States, such as the cultural Pan-Africanism of the Civil Rights and Black Power movements which emphasized the adoption of African customs in names, clothing, music and hairstyles. She describes the new Pan-Africanism as rooted in a diasporic consciousness as well as a growing awareness among immigrants of the significance of racism in the United States and the need to develop political alliances in response to it: "Experiences of racism and to some extent classism lead some African immigrants to bond with other Africans, African Americans and Afro-Caribbeans in order to achieve the access to educational, income and occupational resources that are vital to their mobility in the United States" (2012: 230).

Thus, with increased time spent in the United States and more exposure to racism, some black immigrants join with African Americans through such movements as the new Pan-Africanism, working together to fight against racism and social injustice. Similarly, in their study of Eastern African immigrants in Minnesota, Guenther, Pendaz and Makene (2011) describe an initial sense of confusion and uncertainty about race among them in their initial exposure to the United States. The immigrants they studied came from societies divided by clan, ethnicity, and religion, rather than race. Thus, at least at first, they felt unsure of what to think and how to act when first confronted with racial categories and inequalities. Over time, however, along with experiences of discriminatory treatment, they came to recognize the significance of racism in the United States. For men in particular, the experience of police harassment was a powerful one in generating awareness of racism. A Somali immigrant man they interviewed remarked: "I think racism exists in the U.S. It is not something we can ignore. For example, one thing that happens to me is that whenever police stop me and realize that I am black, even if I did not do anything wrong, they give me a ticket" (2011: 108). In addition to personal experiences of racism, such racially charged events as the shooting of Amadou Diallo have also brought black immigrant and black American communities together. When Diallo, an unarmed immigrant from Guinea, was shot by a New York City police officer, Africans and African Americans joined together in solidarity at rallies and protests (Blyden 2012: 172).

African Americans and black immigrants have also joined together on issues related to immigration policy, as evidenced by the recently formed Black Alliance for Just Immigration (BAJI) (Blyden 2012). Organizing on the principle that U.S. immigration policy has been "infused with racism" and that "African Americans, with our history of being economically exploited, marginalized and discriminated against, have much in common with people of color who migrate to the United States, documented and undocumented," BAJI strives for an inclusive immigration policy and a Pan-African network to bridge divides between black immigrants and African Americans.[8]

Intermarriage between black immigrants and black Americans has also led to a resurgence of Pan-African ideals. In her study on black intraracial relationships and bicultural families, Msia Kibona Clark defined Pan-Africanism as "a focus on a shared origin, shared history, and cultural linkages between peoples of African descent" and noted that bicultural blacks defined their identities and relationships within such a context (2012: 46). Likewise, in her research on black interethnic relationships in Boston, Regine O. Jackson (2007: 220) suggests that not only are boundaries permeable between black immigrants and black Americans, but that relations between the groups are often amicable. Her research describes couples who challenge the boundaries between black ethnic groups and develop new meanings of blackness.

If African and Caribbean immigrants find themselves reworking their identities in the United States, there is little doubt that black American identity is also being transformed by the increasingly important presence of black immigrants from Africa and the Caribbean. Using the example of Harlem in New York City, Zain Abdullah (2007) has described how the social and cultural landscape of traditionally black American neighborhoods is being shaped by the major influx since the 1990s of African immigrants. A street sign that reads "African Square" marks a major intersection in Harlem, on the corner of 125th Street and 7th Avenue. And open-air sidewalk stores that are organized like traditional West African markets have become part of the neighborhood's landscape. The area's businesses, such as African hair-braiding salons that are staffed by West African women, draw a wide range of customers, including many black Americans. Abdullah notes how these neighborhood arenas are focal points of routine informal interactions between African immigrants and longtime black American residents. In the course of these encounters what it means to be "black," "African," and "American" all become points of reflection and negotiation.

In sum, research suggests that many different factors underlie the development of black identities, including class, inter-state histories, citizenship status, generation, and gender. Contemporary populations of black immigrants may at least initially try to resist being lumped together with black Americans in order to avoid the attendant stigmas of this identity. African and Caribbean immigrants may try to set themselves apart from black Americans and emphasize their ethnic identity. Over time, however, with lengthened exposure to the United States and the experiences of racism that it brings, there is the development of a greater sense of shared interests with black Americans (Apraku 1996; Foner 2003; Itzigsohn and Dore-Cabral 2000). All of this is not to say that ethnic and other place-of-origin affiliations and communities recede in importance for African and Caribbean immigrants. It is rather that they come to coincide with an emerging sense of shared predicament with black Americans.

For many contemporary immigrants, particularly those from Africa, negotiations of race and blackness are further compounded by religion. This is perhaps especially so in the case of African immigrants who are Muslim, as we explore in the section that follows.

Religion and Identity Formations: The Case of Muslim Immigrants

Scholars have long observed the important role played by religion and religious institutions in the experiences of immigrants; this is particularly the case in the United States, a country with high levels of religiosity. Religion is generally accepted and indeed expected to play an important role in immigrant life. As Raymond Williams writes: "In the U.S., religion is the social category with clearest meaning and acceptance in the host society, so the emphasis on religious affiliation is one of the strategies that allows the immigrant to maintain self identity while simultaneously acquiring community acceptance" (1988: 29). In the United States, then, immigrants are expected to participate in religious institutions.

In the contemporary era, Islam and its adherents have become a notable target of stigma in the United States. The political context of the War on Terror has led Muslims to become a particular focus of suspicion, policing, and hostility. As we have described in Chapter Two, especially since 9/11, the image of the "terrorist alien" has helped to organize the U.S. immigration regime and its policies of enforcement. Muslims have found themselves to be a particular target of suspicion and focus in the era of immigration enforcement. In 2001, the U.S. Department of Justice recorded a 1,600 percent increase in anti-Muslim hate crimes from the prior year, and these numbers rose 10 percent between 2005 and 2006. The Council on American-Islamic Relations processed 2,647 civil rights complaints in 2006, a 25 percent increase from the prior year and a 600 percent increase since 2000 (Read 2008).

Noting the above conditions, scholars have argued that Muslims are undergoing racialization. Muslims, they suggest, have found themselves to be stigmatized on the basis of a presumption of intrinsic difference and inferiority *as Muslims*. In making this point, Taras (2013) describes Islamophobia, or hostility toward Islam and Muslims, as "a cryptic articulation of the concepts of race and racism even if overtly it appears as a form of religious-based prejudice" (422).

These processes of stigmatization are complicated by the heterogeneity of Muslim immigrants as a population. Muslim Americans are a profoundly diverse population, encompassing persons of African, Asian, European, and Middle Eastern descent who have unique histories and cultural traditions. They originate from more than eighty countries on four continents. Nearly one-third are South Asian, one-third are Arab, one-fifth are U.S.-born black Muslims (mainly converts), and a small but growing number are U.S.-born Anglo and Hispanic converts. While the majority (about two-thirds) are immigrants to the United States, second- and third-generation, U.S.-born Americans are increasingly numerous (Read 2008).

Given this diversity, some observers have emphasized the fluidity and variability of Muslim stigmatization. That is, the strength and character of this stigmatization is experienced differently by different Muslim Americans. Besides social class, racial designation and skin color are particularly important. If those of African descent are likely to find themselves labeled as "black," Middle Easterners may be seen as "white," and South Asians as straddling "Asian" and "white." Accordingly, in terms of official classifications and phenotype, the racial classifications of Muslims are both heterogeneous and fluid, defying simple generalization.

As Zareena Grewal (2009) notes in her study of college-educated Muslim Americans, however, an active identification with Islam, especially when accompanied by such markers as the hijab or headscarf, has the potential to overshadow the significance of diversity among Muslim Americans. One of her interviewees, a white American convert named Janet, spoke of how her use of the hijab had introduced her to experiences of discrimination. Even as she continued to identify as white, she also noted that her phenotype did not protect her from the particular stigmas of a Muslim identity. Her experience of being seen as a foreigner and a traitor point to the significance of the "terrorist alien" image of Muslims in the United States:

Of course I know I'm still white and [Muslims] think of me as white but in my head I really identify myself as a minority now. . . . [Because of my scarf] other white Americans don't see me as white. They are always trying to figure out this imaginary accent and before this *hijab* [scarf] nobody used to ask me where I was born. . . .When I [say] Detroit, they [are] confused. A lot of white people see me as a traitor. . . . so that makes me identify much more as a Muslim than as white. I have to worry about discrimination like any other minority; I stick out in crowds. . . . How am I any whiter than a Syrian girl with blue eyes? (Grewal 2009: 329)

The complex interactions of Muslim stigma with racial assign-ment are explored by Ajrouch and Kusow (2007) in a comparative analysis of Muslim immigrants from Somalia and the Middle East. They show that for Middle Eastern immigrants who are labeled by others as racially "white," Muslim status can serve to "darken" identity. That is, being Muslim reduces the significance and atten-dant privileges of being white. However, for the black Somali Muslim immigrants she studied, the situation is more complicated as the stigmas of "black," "Muslim," and immigrant status coa-lesce in powerful ways to produce strengthened exclusion from the larger white society. If religion was experienced as a source of stigma and marginalization by Somali immigrants, however, it was also a strategic resource. As we have described in our discus-sion of African immigrant identities, Ajrouch and Kusow (2007) found the Somali immigrants purposefully using their religion at times to differentiate themselves from black Americans, in an effort to avoid identification with them.

Indeed, one way in which Muslim stigma is shaping Muslim immigrant identities is by enhancing a sense of religious solidar-ity. The post 9/11 era has been widely observed to be a time of rising levels of religious identification and involvement for Muslim Americans. There has also been a growth of political conscious-ness and engagement as they have mobilized in response to the backlash against them, becoming more involved in U.S. politics (Abdo 2006; Cainkar 2004; Kibria 2011). These trends have led some to suggest that Muslims are undergoing ethnogenesis, merging into a pan-ethnic religious group that also becomes a basis for integration into U.S. society. They are, in short, becom-ing Muslim Americans. This scenario is deeply challenged by the tremendous diversity of the Muslim American population, however, as we have described earlier. As a heavily first-generation immigrant population, identities based on place of origin continue to organize the lives of many Muslim Americans.

Studies of Muslim immigrant communities do also show important identity shifts. Grewal (2009) describes how college-educated second-generation Muslim Americans may reject their parents' preference that they marry endogamously, to a Muslim from their own ethno-national group. Instead, they saw their pool of potential marriage partners to be composed of Muslims from many ethno-national backgrounds. The question of race and skin color was a particularly thorny one in intergenerational relations, with the immigrant parents often expressing a desire that their children marry those of lighter skin color. Grewal (2009) describes the resulting intergenerational dialogue as part of a larger process of racial identity negotiations in these communities.

The experiences of Muslim Americans as we have described highlight the complexity and fluidity of racial formations as they intersect with religious identity. The stigmatization of Muslims has generated a renewed interest in the potential role of religion in processes of racial formation.

Conclusions: Immigrant Identities and Racial Formations

This chapter has explored how Latino/as, Asian Americans, and black immigrants find a sense of belonging and identity as they navigate the racial boundaries of the United States. Immigrants from Latin America, Asia, the Caribbean, and Africa confront a black-white racial order that may be quite different from the social hierarchies of their sending countries, where, in some cases, other elements such as ethnicity, class, and religion overshadow the significance of race as an aspect of social inequality. As they face the racial landscape of the United States, immigrants strive to find meaningful affiliations and to use available opportunities to situate themselves in favorable positions. As they do so they may turn to the transnational arena as a source of social capital and psychological support. They may also strive to differentiate themselves from African Americans and other oppressed groups in an effort to avoid the stigmas of these associations. Concurrently, immigrants may create alliances with other racial minorities to participate in shared struggles against racism and injustice. These varied and shifting identity strategies highlight the dynamic character of racialization, in which immigrants both shape and are shaped by race. In their seminal work, Robert Miles and Malcolm Brown note that "the process of racialization of human beings entails the racialization of the processes in which they participate and the structures and institutions that result" (2003[1989]: 76).

If our analysis highlights the dynamic and ongoing nature of immigrant identity formations, we also show the continued significance of race as part of the fundamental context in which these developments take place. Immigrants from Africa and the Caribbean face the specific dilemmas of racialization as "black", and Latino/a and Asian immigrants are racialized as "outsiders" in America, whether as criminals, terrorists, competitors, or model minorities. As suggested by these examples, the pan-ethnic categories of "Asian American," "black," and "Latino/a" have been important, albeit contested, foci of racialization for immigrants in the contemporary era. Even as these categories have been the basis for important political mobilizations of pan-ethnic solidarity, they have also been at the heart of racial meanings and stigma.

Analysts of the United States often note the potential for the development of a fundamentally new kind of racial order in the aftermath of the Immigration and Nationality Act of 1965 which brought diverse populations of immigrants into the country. In fact, as we have seen, many new immigrants do not seem to neatly fit into the categories of "black" and "white", and so bring the notion of a simple dichotomy of racial dominance and oppression into question. But rather than suggesting the emergence of a "post-racial" society, as some have argued, we see these developments in relation to the ongoing formation and reformation of race. Even as groups like Latino/as and Asian Americans complicate the notions of black-white polarity that have defined the U.S. racial order, their incorporation remains anchored in the persistent dynamics of white privilege. Racial conditions continue to undergird processes of immigrant incorporation powerfully, albeit in ways that are perhaps more opaque than in previous times. As the Sri Lankan theorist of race Ambalavaner Sivanandan has eloquently noted: "Racism never stands still. It changes shape, size, contours, purpose, function, with changes in the economy, the social structure, the system and above all, the challenges, the resistances, to that system" (1989: 85–90).

Conclusions

Race, Immigration, and the American Dream

If they are sober, industrious, and frugal, they soon become Masters, establish themselves in Business, marry, raise families, and become respectable Citizens.

> Benjamin Franklin, *Information to Those Who Would Remove to America*, 1794, p. 13

My mother, Maud Ariel McKoy, [arrived in America] from Jamaica aboard the motor ship *Turialba* in 1923. My father, Luther Powell, had arrived three years earlier at the Port of Philadelphia. They met in New York City, married, became Americans and raised a family. By their hard work and their love for this country, they enriched this nation and helped it grow and thrive. They instilled in their children and grandchildren that same love of country and a spirit of optimism. My family's story is a common one that has been told by millions of Americans. We are a land of immigrants.

> Colin Powell, "The America I Believe In," 2005

From Benjamin Franklin in the late eighteenth century to Colin Powell in the twenty-first century, the national leaders of the United States have drawn on the inspiring rhetoric of the American Dream in their statements. The American Dream portrays the United States as a land of opportunity, a nation where the hopes and aspirations of virtuous individuals can come true. These are ideas that have been at the heart of U.S. nation-building and its projects of global hegemony and empire.

The American Dream is a deeply entrenched nationalist

ideology, resilient in the face of the many contradictory realities that surround it. There is little doubt that racial inequality has constituted one of the greatest challenges to the credibility of the American Dream and its promise of opportunity for all. In August 1963, Martin Luther King, Jr., spoke eloquently of a vision of racial equality, of an America in which children would be judged "not by the color of their skin but by the content of their character." His speech was a defining moment of the Civil Rights movement, which advanced the cause of racial equality in the United States.

For some Americans, the rise to political power in the twenty-first century of President Barack Obama, the country's first black President, has come to symbolize the fact of an America that may have had a racist past but is now free of race. There are many important ways, however, in which even half a century after his famous "I have a Dream" speech, King's vision of racial inequality remains unrealized in important respects. Though the black middle class has expanded since the 1960s, it is also the case that the white middle class is far more advantaged, in terms of occupation, income, residential patterns, and other resources (Pattillo-McCoy 1999). In general, evidence abounds of sharp disparities in the life chances and circumstances of black and white Americans. The median wealth of white households is twenty times that of black households (Pew Research Center 2009). Blacks are twice as likely to be unemployed, three times more likely to live in poverty and more than six times as likely to be imprisoned compared with whites (Urban League 2009).

How do we explain the resilience as nationalist ideology of the American Dream, of its ability to smooth over the often harsh realities of inequality, especially those of race, in the United States? In what follows we consider the role of immigration in sustaining the idea of the American Dream. Our discussion highlights a conceptual theme of this book: the race–immigration nexus. We have defined this as a fluid and intertwined bundle of linkages between race and immigration, specifically between the institutions, ideologies and practices that define these areas.

Conclusions

Immigrants and the American Dream

In 1965, the United States passed the Immigration and Nationality Act, departing from the overtly discriminatory national-origins laws that had guided immigration in previous decades. Since that time, the United States has experienced an influx of immigrants, many from Asia and Latin America. Immigration has continued at a steady pace, even in the face of conditions that seem countervailing, such as the global economic recession of the early twenty-first century. The persistence of immigration reflects deep-seated conditions, including an ongoing demand for immigrant labor in the U.S. economy. As these immigration flows occur, they strengthen the image of America as a highly desirable destination, thereby fortifying the ideology of the American Dream. In other words, that so many women and men want to come to America offers proof positive that it remains, as it has always been, an exceptional nation, unparalleled in its freedom and opportunities. Media reports and political statements deploy images of immigrants flooding the gates, perhaps risking life and limb just for the chance to get into the promised land of America. The border control activities of the United States have also been part of the construction of these imageries of a prized destination. The late twentieth and early twenty-first century has been a time of enormous expansion of the U.S. apparatus of immigration control and security. There is a symbolic dimension to this expansion, in addition to its many other consequences. The politics of building better fences on the border affirms the American Dream. It is precisely because of its exceptionalism, its greatness, that the United States needs to expend so much on defending its borders against immigrants.

In the spring of 2013, following the election to a second term of President Obama, the United States seemed poised to legislate immigration reform. Along with a general bipartisan consensus among Democrats and Republicans about the need for reform, there was also vigorous disagreement and heated debate about how best to achieve this goal. The American Dream figured prominently, organizing an underlying discourse of "good" and "bad" immigrants. Those taking a generally positive stance on immigration drew on the American Dream to articulate notions of the "good immigrant." For example, arguments in favor of more high-skilled immigration asserted the need for the United States to retain its competitive edge in the global economy by attracting the best and brightest from around the world. These "good immigrants" would ensure that America retained its exceptionalism, its promise of greatness. On the opposite side, those advocating a highly restrictive approach spoke of the need to preserve the American Dream by protecting the country from immigrants, especially "bad immigrants." The rhetoric here was of how immigrants threatened the integrity and viability of the American Dream by heightening if not creating problems such as crime, violence, overpopulation, pollution, unemployment, and the abundance of jobs with poor working conditions. In short, across these extremely diverse strands, the political discourse of immigration in the United States has had a constant ideological thread—that of the American Dream and its related notions of "good" and "bad" immigrants.

Given the importance of the American Dream as a signifier of political legitimacy, it is not surprising that immigrants themselves have been observed to evoke it in their narratives of coming to America (Hochschild 1996; Kibria 2011). Through an expressed belief in the American Dream, immigrants strive to be "good immigrants." To be sure, frustration and disillusionment with life in America are also critical features of the immigrant experience. However, the American Dream can inform immigrant efforts to claim "American-ness," as they turn to it to legitimate their presence in the United States and their identity as Americans. The ideals of the American Dream can also be a source of comfort to immigrants, enabling them to cope with the hardships and degradations of life in the United States by giving them hope that with hard work, the future will indeed be better. It is also important to note the particular role that immigrants can play in the transnational cultivation of the American Dream. The American Dream is not only a national ideology, but also a global one. It is disseminated around the world through a globalized culture of mass consumption and media. Building on these trends, immigrants may endorse an "American Dream image" of the United States within their societies of origin. This is especially so for immigrants from the global South, who derive status and prestige in their communities of origin from their residence in the United States.

The notion of "good" and "bad" immigrants that has marked political discourse on immigration in the United States is also part of the country's racial landscape. We would argue that the good immigrant–bad immigrant framework has played an important role in masking the racial inequalities that undergird the American Dream. The negative positioning of black Americans in relation to immigrants has been a consistent theme in United States history. As we have discussed, in the contemporary low-wage sectors of the U.S. economy, employers deploy notions of immigrants as "good workers" in ways that enhance the stigmatization of unskilled black American workers. And the pervasive stereotype of Asian Americans as a "model minority" has contributed to "color-blind" ideas that argue that racial discrimination no longer exists. The reasoning is that since Asians are a racial minority who are able to be successful, racial discrimination is not responsible for the disadvantages of black Americans. In a neoliberal era of government deregulation and cuts on social service spending, these notions have served to legitimate the withdrawal of state responsibility for addressing racial inequalities.

Among the notable features of the good immigrant–bad immigrant concept, however, is its pendulum-like quality. As highlighted by the history of Asian Americans, those who are seen as members of a "model minority" can also rapidly become a "perilous minority," depending on the circumstances. There is, in short, a marked quality of fluidity to these constructions. The vilification of immigrants can serve to unify nativist forces across racial lines. In an era of "color-blind" ideology, when it is normatively important to disavow racism, the explicit targeting of persons based on their "foreignness" rather than their skin color has been a prevalent strategy of nativist movements. In the contemporary era, the "illegal alien" and "the terrorist alien" have been important foci of public anger and resentment in the United States. Seen in this light, the targeting of immigrants can create a certain sense of nationalist racial unity as captured by the idea that all Americans, regardless of the color of their skin, are united against enemies from outside. Rather than aiming to remedy racial inequalities, political attention comes to focus on fighting the foreign threat.

Notes

Chapter 1: The Race–Immigration Nexus

1 http://www.whitehouse.gov/the-press-office/2013/01/29/remarks-president-comprehensive-immigration-reform

2 Emma Lazarus, "The New Colossus," quoted in Alan M. Kraut, *The Huddled Masses: The Immigrant in American Society, 1880–1921,* 2nd ed. (Wheeling, IL: Harlan Davidson 2001), 2.

3 J. Hector St. John de Crèvecoeur, *Letters from an American Farmer* (London, 1782), reproduced in Moses Rischin, *Immigration and the American Tradition* (Indianapolis: Bobbs-Merrill, 1876), 25–26.

4 For example, the U.S. Census Bureau reports that in 2010, the median household income for whites (non-Hispanic) was $54,620 compared to $32,068 for Blacks. At 27.4 percent, poverty rates for blacks were also far higher than that of 9.9 percent for whites. http://www.census.gov/newsroom/releases/archives/income_wealth/cb11–157.html#tablea. Also, as reported by the Centers for Disease Control and Prevention, negative health disparities between African Americans and other Americans are striking and are apparent in life expectancy, infant mortality, and other measures of health status. For example, in 1999 the average American could expect to live 77.8 years, whereas the average African American could only expect to live 73.1 years: http://www.cdc.gov/omhd/populations/BAA/BAA.htm

5 Executive summary of *Economic Mobility of Immigrants in the United States* by The Brookings Institutions, An Initiative of the Pew Charitable Trusts 2007.

6 Executive summary of *Economic Mobility of Immigrants in the United States* by The Brookings Institutions, An Initiative of the Pew Charitable Trusts 2007, p. 3.

7 These data are featured in the TED article, "Education and occupations of the foreign born in 2011." http://www.bls.gov/opub/ted/2012/ted_20120606.htm

Chapter 2: Immigration Policy and Racial Formations

1 These ideas were part of the nineteenth-century "manifest destiny" ideology that America was destined to expand across the continent as part of its "mission" in the world, to bring democracy and progress to other parts of the world.

2 Countries that were U.S. colonies, such as the Philippines, were exempt from the "Asiatic Barred Zone."

3 The Act had two quota provisions. The first, in effect until 1927, tied the quota calculations to those in the country in 1890. From 1927 to 1952, the quotas were calculated based on U.S. inhabitants in 1920.

4 U.S. Citizenship and Immigration Services, "Legislation from 1901–1940: Immigration Act of May 26, 1924 (43 Statutes-at-large 153)," http://www.uscis.gov/files/nativedocuments/Legislation%20from%201901–1940.pdf

5 http://pewresearch.org/databank/dailynumber/?NumberID=1225

6 http://www.pewhispanic.org/2011/12/28/as-deportations-rise-to-record-levels-most-latinos-oppose-obamas-policy/

7 http://www.nytimes.com/2012/07/29/opinion/sunday/migrants-freedom-ride.html?_r=2&ref=immigrationandemigration
http://colorlines.com/archives/2012/08/riding_for_justice_undoubus_heads_to_the_dnc.html

8 http://www.whitehouse.gov/sites/default/files/omb/legislative/sap/112/saphr6429r_20121128.pdf

9 The policy applies only to those who entered the United States before the age of sixteen, were under the age of thirty as of the June 15 announcement, and have continuously resided in the United States for the past five years. They also must either be enrolled in school, have graduated from high school, obtained a GED, or been honorably discharged from the military or Coast Guard. In addition, they must not have been convicted of a felony, a significant misdemeanor, or at least three misdemeanors. See: http://www.dhs.gov/ynews/releases/20120612-napolitano-announces-deferred-action-process-for-young-people.shtm

10 http://www.migrationpolicy.org/news/2012_06_15.php

11 According to a USA TODAY/Gallup Poll, 8 in 10 Latinos approved of the President's directive (Page 2012).

12 http://www.washingtonpost.com/politics/exit-poll-6-in-10-voters-in-presidential-election-call-economy-biggest-issue-facing-country/2012/11/06/d1c771b0-286f-11e2-aaa5-ac786110c486_story.html

Chapter 3: Race and the Occupational Strategies of Immigrants

1 http://www.nytimes.com/2008/03/16/nyregion/nyregionspecial2/16Rdinersnj.html

2 For more information on recent landmark cases dealing with racial bias in firefighters' promotional tests see Adam Liptak, 2009, *New York Times Online*. "New Scrutiny of Judge's Most Controversial Case." http://www.nytimes.com/2009/06/06/us/politics/06ricci.html

3 In framing U.S. colonial pursuits in the Philippines, proponents claimed that U.S. colonial programs were different from traditional European imperialism. Julian Go describes how such proponents argued that "unlike European empires, the U.S. enterprise was an exercise in effective benevolence, bringing to those whom it touched the benefits of Anglo-American civilization." Julian Go, "Introduction: Global Perspectives on the U.S. Colonial State in the Philippines," in *The American Colonial State in the Philippines: Global Perspectives*, ed. Julian Go and Anne L. Foster (Durham, NC: Duke University Press, 2003), p. 2.

4 Quoted in Choy 2003: 20–1.

5 Despite shortages of trained nursing personnel in rural areas in the Philippines that nursing school graduates could potentially fill, the pull factor of wages in the U.S. outweighs calls to stay in the Philippines. Additionally, the Philippines' government actively supported nurse migration as a viable economic export that would bring guaranteed remittances. Therefore, nurses and doctors were often applauded for their efforts abroad. In *The Potent Lever of Toil: Nursing Development and Exportation in the Postcolonial Philippines*, Brush notes, "Inadequate wages and high patient-to-nurse ratios, along with reports that the top graduates of Philippines nursing programs, the country's most seasoned nurses, and physicians are migrating abroad, create anxiety that care rendered to the local populace, especially those in rural communities, is in the hands of lesser experienced, lesser qualified personnel" (2010: 1579).

6 Dual labor market theorists have also noted the stratification of the primary and secondary markets into upper and lower tiers (see Hudson 2007).

7 http://fiscalpolicy.org/immigrant-small-business-owners-FPI-20120614.pdf

8 http://www.nytimes.com/2012/07/16/nyregion/union-efforts-over-conditions-at-greengrocers-splits-2-immigrant-groups.html?ref=immigrationandemigration

9 England and Folbre (1999: 40) define care work to include "any occupation in which the worker provides a service to someone with whom he or she is in personal (usually face-to-face) contact. The work is called 'caring' on the assumption that the work responds to a need or desire that is directly expressed by the recipient."

10 Figure taken from Urban (2009: 265), who cites Lucy Maynard Salmon, *Domestic Service* (New York: Macmillan) 1901: 54–62.

11 Drawn from the title of Noel Ignatiev's 1995 book called *How the Irish Became White*.

12 The Great Migration refers to the early twentieth century movement of

millions of African Americans in the rural South to the Northeast, West and other regions of the country.

13 In her research, Pei-Chia Lan (2002) explains the importance of the tradition of filial piety in Chinese families. She writes: "Child rearing is viewed as a process of social investment with an expectation of delayed repayment, or in Chinese, *bau-da* (payback). Parents undergo economic and emotional costs in bearing and raising children, this tradition stipulates, so children, especially sons, are obligated to return the debts through provision of care for their aging parents" (169).

14 http://www.domesticworkers.org/homeeconomics/key-findings

15 http://www.nytimes.com/2012/11/27/business/a-study-of-home-help-finds-low-worker-pay-and-few-benefits.html

16 http://articles.latimes.com/2012/feb/10/local/la-me-nannies-20120207

17 http://www.labor.ny.gov/legal/laws/pdf/domestic-workers/about-domestic-workers-law.pdf

Chapter 4: Immigrant Identities and Racial Hierarchies

1 http://www.whitehouse.gov/the-press-office/2013/01/29/remarks-president-comprehensive-immigration-reform

2 In the late nineteenth and early twentieth centuries there was a movement of men from the state of Punjab to the U.S., especially to California and Washington, as there was a demand for railroad and farm laborers. However, due to discriminatory naturalization and immigration laws, the population dwindled such that by 1940 only an estimated 2,400 Asian Indians remained in the country (Kibria 2006: 206).

3 Internment Archives, Document 00055, Page 002. Retrieved March 13, 2013. http://www.internmentarchives.com/showdoc.php?docid=00055&search_id=19269&pagenum=2

4 In the following section the terms Caribbean, Afro-Caribbean, and West Indian are used interchangeably. Because of our focus on the intersection of race and immigration, we focus on those Caribbean populations that identify as black. Additionally, in accordance with the American Sociological Association Style Guide (fourth ed.), we do not capitalize "black" in our discussion of black Americans and black immigrants.

5 These occupation statistics from the U.S. Census Bureau 2009 American Community Survey include all foreign-born African immigrants, regardless of reported race (McCabe 2011).

6 Despite attempts at intraracial solidarity across ethnic borders, Garvey failed to achieve a successful solidarity movement. Vickerman notes that Garvey's exclusion and suspicion of light-skinned blacks in favor of a racial solidarity based on dark skin intensified conflict between African Americans and black immigrant groups. Garvey, Vickerman explains, based his movement on the

Jamaican-born perception that light-skinned blacks had more power and resources than dark-skinned blacks (Vickerman 1999: 93).

7 For more information on the historical ties between the United States and Liberia, see Hana E. Brown (2011:152), "Refugees, Rights, and Race: How Legal Status Shapes Liberian Immigrants' Relationship with the State."

8 http://www.blackalliance.org/mission-and-history/

References

Abdo, Geneive. 2006. *Mecca and Main Street: Muslim Life in America After 9/11*. New York: Oxford University Press.

Abdullah, Zain. 2009. "African 'Soul Brothers' in "Hood: Immigration, Islam, and the Black Encounter." *Anthropological Quarterly* 82(1): 37–62.

Abelmann, Nancy, and John Lie. 1995. *Blue Dreams: Korean Americans and Los Angeles Riots*. Cambridge, MA: Harvard University Press.

Adler, Rachel H. 2005. "Oye Compadre! The Chef Needs a Dishwasher: Yucatecan Men in the Dallas Restaurant Economy." *Urban Anthropology and Studies of Cultural Systems and World Economic Development* 34: 217–46.

Ajrouch, Kristine J., and Abdi Kusow. 2007. "Racial and Religious Contexts: Situational Identities among Lebanese and Somali Muslim Immigrants." *Ethnic and Racial Studies* 30: 72–94.

Alba, Richard. 1990. *Ethnic Identity: The Transformation of White America*. New Haven: Yale University Press.

Alba, Richard, and Victor Nee. 2003. *Remaking the American Mainstream: Assimilation and Contemporary Immigration*. Cambridge, MA: Harvard University Press.

Alberts, Heike C., and Helen D. Hazen. 2005. " 'There Are Always Two Voices . . .': International Students' Intentions to Stay in the United States or Return to Their Home Countries." *International Migration* 43(3): 131–54.

Apraku, Kofi Konadu. 1996. *Outside Looking In: An African Perspective on American Pluralistic Society*. Westport, CT: Praeger.

Arthur, John A. 2000. *Invisible Sojourners: African Immigrant Diaspora in the United States*. Westport, CT: Praeger.

Attewell, Paul, and David E. Lavin. 2007. *Passing the Torch: Does Higher Education for the Disadvantaged Pay Off Across the Generations?* New York: Russell Sage Foundation.

Bakalian, Anny, and Medhi Bozorgmehr. 2009. *Backlash 9/11: Middle Eastern and Muslim Americans Respond*. Berkeley: University of California Press.

References

Balogun, Oluwakemi M. 2011. "No Necessary Tradeoff: Context, Life Course, and Social Networks in the Identity Formation of Second-Generation Nigerians in the USA." *Ethnicities* 11: 436–66.

Basch, Linda, Nina Glick Schiller, and Cristina Szanton Blanc. 2008. "Transnational Projects: A New Perspective." In *The Transnational Studies Reader: Intersections and Innovations*, ed. Sanjeev Khagram and Peggy Levitt. New York: Routledge, pp. 261–72.

Bashi, Vilna Francine. 2007. *Survival of the Knitted: Immigrant Social Networks in a Stratified World*. Stanford, CA: Stanford University Press.

Batalova, Jeanne, and B. Lindsay Lowell. 2006. " 'The Best and the Brightest': Immigrant Professionals in the U.S." In *The Human Face of Global Mobility: International Highly Skilled Migration in Europe, North America and the Asia-Pacific*, ed. M. P. Smith and A. Favell. New Brunswick, NJ: Transaction Publishers, pp. 81–101.

Batalova, Jeanne, and Michael Fix. 2008. *Uneven Progress: The Employment Pathways of Skilled Immigrants in the United States*. With Peter A. Creticos. Washington, D.C.: Migration Policy Institute.

Baum, Bruce. 2006. *The Rise and Fall of the Caucasian Race: A Political History of Racial Identity*. New York: New York University Press.

Bean, Frank D., and Gillian Stevens. 2003. *America's Newcomers and the Dynamics of Diversity*. New York: Russell Sage Foundation.

Benson, Janel E. 2006. "Exploring the Racial Identities of Black Immigrants in the United States." *Sociological Forum* 21: 219–47.

Bhalla, Vibha. 2010. "We Wanted to End Disparities at Work: Physician Migration, Racialization and a Struggle for Equality." *Journal of American Ethnic History* 29, 3: 40–78.

Black Alliance for Just Immigration. 2013. "Mission and History." Retrieved March 19, 2013. http://www.blackalliance.org/mission-and-history/

Blyden, Nemata. 2012. "Relationships Among Blacks in the Diaspora: African and Caribbean Immigrants and American-Born Blacks." In *Africans in Global Migration: Searching for Promised Lands*, ed. J. A. Arthur, J. Takougang, and T. Owusu. North America: Lexington Books, pp. 161–74.

Boggioni, Joshua A. 2009. "Unofficial Americans—What To Do with Undocumented Students: An Argument Against Suppressing the Mind." *The University of Toledo Law Review* 40, 2: 453–86.

Bonacich, Edna. 1973. "A Theory of Middleman Minorities," *American Sociological Review* 38: 583–94.

Bonacich, Edna, and John Modell. 1980. *The Economic Basis of Ethnic Solidarity: Small Businesses in the Japanese American Community*. Berkeley: University of California Press.

Bonilla-Silva, Eduardo. 1999. "The Essential Social Fact of Race." *American Sociological Review* 64, 6: 899–906.

References

———. 2003. *Racism without Racists: Colorblind Racism and the Persistence of Racial Inequality in the United States.* Lanham, MD: Rowman & Littlefield.

———. 2004. "From Bi-Racial to Tri-Racial: Towards a New System of Racial Stratification in the USA." *Ethnic and Racial Studies* 27: 931–50.

Borjas, George. 1990. *Friends or Strangers? The Impact of Immigrants on the U.S. Economy.* New York: Basic Books.

Bowles, Samuel, and Herbert Gintis. 1976. *Schooling in Capitalist America: Education Reform and the Contradictions of Economic Life.* New York: Basic Books.

Branch, Enobong Hannah, and Melissa E. Wooten. 2012. "Suited for Service: Racialized Rationalizations for the Ideal Domestic Servant from the Nineteenth to the Early Twentieth Century." *Social Science History* 36, 2: 169–89.

Brodkin, Karen. 2002. *How Jews Became White Folks and What That Says about Race in America.* New Brunswick, NJ: Rutgers University Press.

Brown, Hana E. 2011. "Refugees, Rights, and Race: How Legal Status Shapes Liberian Immigrants' Relationship with the State." *Social Problems* 58, 1: 144–63.

Brush, Barbara L. 2010. "The Potent Lever of Toil: Nursing Development and Exportation in the Postcolonial Philippines." *American Journal of Public Health* 100, 9: 1572–81.

Brush, Barbara L., Julie Sochalski, and Anne M. Berger. 2004. "Imported Care: Recruiting Foreign Nurses To U.S. Health Care Facilities." *Health Affairs* 23, 3: 78–87.

Cainkar, Louise. 2004. "Islamic Revival Among Second-Generation Arab-America Muslims: The American Experience and Globalization Intersect." *Bulletin of the Royal Institute for Inter-Faith Studies* 6, 2: 99–120.

Camarillo, Albert M. 2007. "Mexico." In *The New Americans: A Guide to Immigration Since 1965,* ed. Mary C. Waters & Reed Ueda with Helen B. Marrow. Cambridge, MA: Harvard University Press.

Cantor, Guillermo, 2010. "Struggling for Immigrants' Rights at the Local Level: The Domestic Workers Bill of Rights Initiative in a Suburb of Washington, D.C." *Journal of Ethnic and Migration Studies* 36, 7:1061–78.

Capps, Randy, Kristen McCabe, and Michael Fix. 2011. *New Streams: Black African Migration to the United States.* Washington, D.C: Migration Policy Institute.

Carter, Bob, Marci Green, and Rick Halpern. 1996. "Immigration Policy and the Racialization of Migrant Labour: The Construction of National Identity in the USA and Britain" *Ethnic and Racial Studies* 19, 1: 135–57.

Chakravartty, Paula. 2006. "Symbolic Analysts or Indentured Servants? Indian High-Tech Migrants in America's Information Economy." In *The Human Face of Global Mobility: International Highly Skilled Migration in Europe, North America and the Asia-Pacific,* ed. M. P. Smith and A. Favell. New Brunswick, NJ: Transaction Publishers, pp.159–80.

References

Chishti, Muzaffar, and Faye Hipsman. 2012. "Key Factors, Unresolved Issues in New Deferred Action Program for Immigrant Youth Will Determine Its Success." Washington, D.C: *Migration Policy Institute*, http://www.migration-information.org/USFocus/display.cfm?ID=903

Chisti, Muzaffar, Doris Meissner, and Claire Bergeron. 2011. "At Its 25th Anniversary, IRCA Lives On." Washington, D.C: *Migration Policy Institute*, http://www.migrationinformation.org/USFocus/display.cfm?ID=861

Choy, Catherine Ceniza. 2003. *Empire of Care: Nursing and Migration in Filipino American History*. Durham, NC: Duke University Press.

———. 2007. "Philippines." In *The New Americans: A Guide to Immigration Since 1965*, ed. M.C. Waters, R. Ueda, and H. B. Marrow. Cambridge, MA: Harvard University Press, pp. 556–70.

Clark, Msia Kibona. 2012. "Identity Formation and Integration Among Bicultural Immigrant Blacks." In *Africans in Global Migration: Searching for Promised Lands*, ed. J. A. Arthur, J. Takougang, and T. Owusu. Lanham, MD: Lexington Books, pp. 45–66.

Cornell, Stephen, and Douglas Hartmann. 1998. *Ethnicity and Race: Making Identities in a Changing World*. Thousand Oaks, CA: Pine Forge Press.

Coutin, Susan Bibler. 2005. "Contesting Criminality: Illegal Immigration and the Spatialization of Legality." *Theoretical Criminology* 9, 1: 5–33.

Cranford, Cynthia. 2005. "Networks of Exploitation: Immigrant Labor and the Restructuring of the Los Angeles Janitorial Industry." *Social Problems* 52, 3: 379–97.

Daniels, Roger. 2004. *Guarding the Golden Door: American Immigration Policy and Immigrants since 1882*. New York: Hill and Wang.

Davis, F. James. 1991. *Who Is Black? One Nation's Definition*. University Park, PA: Penn State University Press.

De Genova, Nicholas. 2005. *Working the Boundaries: Race, Space, and "Illegality" in Mexican Chicago*. Durham, NC: Duke University Press.

———. 2012. "The 'War on Terror' as Racial Crisis: Homeland Security, Obama, and Racial (Trans)Formations." In *Racial Formation in the Twenty-First Century*, ed. D. HoSang, O. LaBennett, and L. Pulido. Berkeley: University of California Press.

DeSipio, Louis. 2006. "Latino Civic and Political Participation." In "National Research Council (U.S.) Panel on Hispanics in the United States," *Hispanics and the Future of America*, ed. M. Tienda and F. Mitchell. Washington, D.C.: National Academies Press. (http://www.ncbi.nlm.nih.gov/books/NBK19906/)

DeSipio, Louis, and Rodolpho O. de la Garza. 1998. *Making Americans, Remaking America: Immigration and Immigration Policy*. Boulder, CO: Westview Press.

Diamond, Timothy. 1992. *Making Gray Gold: Narratives of Nursing Home Care*. Chicago, IL: University of Chicago Press.

References

Dietrich, David R. 2011. "The Specter of Racism in the 2005–6 Immigration Debate: Preserving Racial Group Position." *Critical Sociology* 38: 723–45.

Do, Anh. 2012. "Filipino Nurses Win Language Discrimination Settlement." *Los Angeles Times*, September 18. Retrieved April 6, 2013, http://articles.latimes.com/2012/sep/18/local/la-me-english-only-20120918

Doeringer, Peter B., and Michael J. Piore. 1971. *Internal Labor Markets and Manpower Analysis*. Armonk, NY: M.E. Sharpe.

Dowling, Julie A., and C. Alison Newby. 2010. "So Far from Miami: Afro-Cuban Encounters with Mexicans in the U.S. Southwest." *Latino Studies* 8, 2: 176.

Dreby, Joanna. 2010. *Divided by Borders: Mexican Migrants and their Children*. Berkeley: University of California Press.

Dwoskin, Elizabeth. 2011. "Why Americans Won't Do Dirty Jobs: Crackdown on Immigrants Leaves Business Owners Struggling with Shortages." *Bloomberg BusinessWeek*. November 11. Retrieved May 9, 2013, http://www.nbcnews.com/id/45246594/ns/business-us_business/t/why-americans-wont-do-dirty-jobs/#.UYuhLJVgoVs

Eckstein, Susan, and Thanh-nghi Nguyen. 2011. "The Making and Transnationalization of an Ethnic Niche: Vietnamese Manicurists." *International Migration Review* 45, 3: 639–74.

Ehrenreich, Barbara, and Arlie R. Hochschild. 2002. "Introduction." In *Global Woman: Nannies, Maids, and Sex Workers in the New Economy*, ed. B. Ehrenreich and A. R. Hochschild. New York: Holt Paperbacks, pp. 1–13.

Eitzen, Stanley. 1971. "Two Minorities: The Jews of Poland and the Chinese of the Philippines." In *Ethnic Conflict and Power: A Cross-National Perspective*, ed. D. Gelfand and R. Lee. New York: John Wiley and Sons.

England, Paula, and Nancy Folbre. 1999. "The Cost of Caring." *Annals of the American Academy of Political and Social Science* 561, 1: 39–51.

Espiritu, Yen Le. 1992. *Asian American Panethnicity: Bridging Institutions and Identities*. Philadelphia, PA: Temple University Press.

———. 2003. *Homebound: Filipino American Lives Across Cultures, Communities, and Countries*. Berkeley: University of California Press.

Executive Office of the President: Office of Management and Budget. 2012. *Statement of Administration Policy: H.R. 6429 – STEM Jobs Act of 2012*. Washington, D.C.: Office of Management and Budget. Also available at http://www.whitehouse.gov/sites/default/files/omb/legislative/sap/112/saphr6429r_20121128.pdf.

FAIR. 2013. "Immigration Issues: E-Verify." *Federation for American Immigration Reform*. Retrieved April 4, 2013. http://www.fairus.org/issue/e-verify?A=SearchResult&SearchID=3984630&ObjectID=5126387&ObjectType=35.

Feliciano, Cynthia, Rennie Lee, and Belinda Robnett. 2011. "Racial Boundaries among Latinos: Evidence from Internet Daters' Racial Preferences." *Social Problems* 58, 2: 189–212.

References

Flippen, Chenoa A. 2012. "Laboring Underground: The Employment Patterns of Hispanic Immigrant Men in Durham, NC." *Social Problems* 59, 1: 21–42.

Florida, Richard. 2007. *The Flight of the Creative Class: The New Global Competition for Talent*. New York: Collins.

Foner, Nancy. 2003. "Immigrants and African Americans: Comparative Perspectives on the New York Experience across Time and Space." In *Host Societies and the Reception of Immigrants*, ed. Jeffrey Reitz. La Jolla, CA: Center for Comparative Immigration Studies, pp. 45–71.

——. 2005. *In a New Land: A Comparative View of Immigration*. New York: New York University Press.

——. 2007. "Engagements across National Borders, Then and Now." *Fordham Law Review* (New Dimensions of Citizenship Symposium) 75: 2483–92.

Fortney, Judith. 1972. "Immigrant Professionals: A Brief Historical Survey." *International Migration Review* 6, 1: 50–62.

Franklin, Benjamin. 1794. *Information to Those Who Would Remove to America*. London: Eighteenth Century Collections. Retrieved March 27, 2013, via Gale: http://find.galegroup.com.ezproxy.bu.edu/ecco/start.do?prodId=ECCO

Fredrickson, George. 2002. *Racism: A Short History*. Princeton, NJ: Princeton University Press.

Fuller, Caitlin. 2011. "Flawed E-Verify Law Would Derail Immigration Reform Efforts, Say Experts." *New America Media*. Retrieved April 4, 2013: http://newamericamedia.org/2011/07/flawed-e-verify-law-will-derail-immigration-reform-efforts-say-experts.php

Gans, Herbert J. 1979. "Symbolic ethnicity: The future of ethnic groups and cultures in America." *Ethnic and Racial Studies* 2, 1: 1–20.

Gentsch, Kerstin, and Douglas Massey. 2011. "Labor Market Outcomes for Legal Mexican Immigrants Under the New Regime of Immigrant Enforcement." *Social Science Quarterly* 92: 875–93.

George, Sheba Mariam. 2005. *When Women Come First: Gender and Class in Transnational Migration*. Berkeley and Los Angeles: University of California Press.

Glazer, Nathan, and David P. Moynihan. 1963. *Beyond the Melting Pot: The Negroes, Puerto Ricans, Jews, Italians, and Irish of New York City*. Cambridge, MA: M.I.T. Press.

Glenn, Evelyn Nakano. 1992. "From Servitude to Service Work: The Historical Continuities of Women's Paid and Unpaid Reproductive Labor." *Signs: Journal of Women in Culture and Society* 18, 1: 1–44.

Go, Julian. 2003. "Introduction: Global Perspectives on the U.S. Colonial State in the Philippines." In *The American Colonial State in the Philippines: Global Perspectives*, ed. J. Go and A. L. Foster. Durham, NC: Duke University Press, pp. 1–42.

References

Golash-Boza, Tanya. 2006. "Dropping the Hyphen? Becoming Latino-(a)-American through Racialized Assimilation." *Social Forces* 85: 27–55.

——. 2009. "Does Whitening Happen? Distinguishing Between Race and Color Labels in an African-Descended Community in Peru." *Social Problems* 57, 1: 138–56.

Gold, Steven J. 2004. "From Jim Crow to Racial Hegemony: Evolving Explanations of Racial Hierarchy." *Ethnic and Racial Studies* 27: 951–68.

——. 2010. *The Store in the Hood: A Century Of Ethnic Businesses and Conflict.* Lanham, MD: Rowman & Littlefield.

Goldberg, David Theo. 1993. *Racist Culture: Philosophy and the Politics of Meaning.* Malden, MA: Blackwell Publishers.

Goldberg, David Theo, Michael Musheno, and Lisa Bower, eds. 2001. *Between Law and Culture: Relocating Legal Studies.* Minneapolis: University of Minnesota Press.

Gonzales, Roberto. 2011. "Learning to be Illegal: Undocumented Youth and Shifting Legal Contexts in the Transition to Adulthood." *American Sociological Review* 76, 4: 602–19.

Gordon, Milton. 1964. *Assimilation in American life: The Role of Race, Religion, and National Origins.* New York: Oxford University Press.

Greeley, Andrew M. 1974. "Religion in a Secular Society." *Social Research* 41, 1: 226–40.

Grewal, Zareena A. 2009. "Marriage in Colour: Race, Religion and Spouse Selection in Four American Mosques." *Ethnic and Racial Studies* 32, 2: 323–45.

Gross, Jeff. 2012. "STEMming the Tide." Massachusetts Immigrant and Refugee Advocacy Coalition. *MIRA* Blog. Retrieved April 3, 2013. http://www.miracoalition.org/en/press-room/easyblog/entry/stemming-the-tide

Guenther, Katja M., Sadie Pendaz, and Fortunata Songora Makene. 2011. "The Impact of Intersecting Dimensions of Inequality and Identity on the Racial Status of Eastern African Immigrants." *Sociological Forum* 26, 1: 98–120.

Hagan, Jacqueline Maria. 2004. "Contextualizing Immigrant Labor Market Incorporation: Legal, Demographic, and Economic Dimensions" *Work and Occupations* 31: 407–23.

Hagan, Jacqueline, Nichola Lowe, and Christian Quingla. 2011. "Skills on the Move: Rethinking the Relationship between Human Capital and Immigrant Labor Market Incorporation." *Work and Occupations* 38, 2: 149–78.

Halter, Marilyn. 2007. "Africa: West" in *The New Americans: A Guide to Immigration since 1965*, ed. Mary C. Waters, Reed Ueda and Helen B. Marrow. Cambridge, MA: Harvard University Press.

Handlin, Oscar. 1951. *The Uprooted: The Epic Story of the Great Migrations that Made the American People.* New York: Little, Brown.

Harrison, Bennett, and Barry Bluestone. 1990. *The Great U-Turn: Corporate Restructuring and the Polarizing of America.* New York: Basic Books.

References

Hayano, David. 1981. Ethnic Identification and Disidentification: Japanese Americans' Views of Chinese Americans. *Ethnic Groups* 3: 157–71.

Herberg, Will. 1960. *Protestant—Catholic—Jew: An Essay in American Religious Sociology.* Chicago, IL: University of Chicago Press.

Higham, John. 1955. *Strangers in the Land: Patterns of American Nativism 1860–1925.* New Brunswick, NJ: Rutgers, The State University.

Hochschild, Arlie. 2001. "The Nanny Chain." *American Prospect,* December 19. Retrieved May 8, 2013, http://prospect.org/article/nanny-chain

Hochschild, Jennifer L. 1996. *Facing Up to the American Dream: Race, Class, and the Soul of the Nation.* Princeton, NJ: Princeton University Press.

Holt, Thomas C. 2000. *The Problem of Race in the 21st Century.* Cambridge, MA: Harvard University Press.

Hondagneu-Sotelo, Pierrette. 2007 [2001]. *Doméstica: Immigrant Workers Cleaning and Caring in the Shadows of Affluence.* Berkeley and Los Angeles: University of California Press.

Hudson, Kenneth. 2007. "The New Labor Market Segmentation: Labor Market Dualism in the New Economy." *Social Science Research* 36: 286–312.

Humes, Karen R., Nicholas A. Jones, and Roberto R. Ramirez. 2011. "Overview of Race and Hispanic Origin: 2010." U.S. Census Bureau. Washington, D.C. http://www.census.gov/prod/cen2010/briefs/c2010br-02.pdf

Huntington, Samuel. 2004. "The Hispanic Challenge." *Foreign Policy* March/April: 30–45.

Ignatiev, Noel. 1995. *How the Irish Became White.* New York: Routledge.

Iceland, John, and Melissa Scopilliti. 2008. "Immigrant Residential Segregation in U.S. Metropolitan Areas, 1990–2000." *Demography* 45, 1: 79–94.

Itzigsohn, Jose. 2004. "The Formation of Latino and Latina Panethnic Identities." In *Not Just Black and White,* ed. Nancy Foner and George M. Fredrickson. New York: Russell Sage Foundation, pp. 197–216.

Itzigsohn, Jose, and Carlos Dore-Cabral, 2000. "Competing Identities? Race, Ethnicity and Panethnicity Among Dominicans in the United States." *Sociological Forum* 15: 225–47.

Jachimowicz, Maia, and Deborah W. Meyers. 2002. *Temporary High-Skilled Migration.* Washington, D.C.: Migration Information Source. Available at http://www.migrationinformation.org/USFocus/display.cfm?ID=69

Jackson, Regine O. 2007. "Beyond Social Distancing: Intermarriage and Ethnic Boundaries among Black Americans in Boston." In *The Other African Americans: Contemporary African and Caribbean Immigrants in the United States,* ed. Y. Shaw-Taylor and S. A. Tuch. Lanham, MD: Rowman & Littlefield, pp. 217–53.

Kalleberg, Arne. 2011. *Good Jobs, Bad Jobs: The Rise of Polarized and Precarious Employment Systems in the United States, 1970s-2000s.* New York: Russell Sage Foundation.

Kang, Miliann. 2003. "The Managed Hand: The Commercialization of Bodies and Emotions in Korean Immigrant-Owned Nail Salons." *Gender and Society* 17: 820–39.

——. 2010. *The Managed Hand: Race, Gender and the Body in Beauty Service Work*. Berkeley: University of California Press.

Kanstroom, Daniel. 2007. *Deportation Nation: Outsiders in American History*. Cambridge, MA: Harvard University Press.

Kaplan, Amy. 1998. "Manifest Domesticity." *American Literature* 70: 581–606.

Kaushal, Neeraj, and Michael Fix. 2006. "The Contributions of High-Skilled Immigrants." *Insight* 16: 1–18.

Kapur, Devesh. 2010. *Diaspora, Development, and Democracy: The Domestic Impact of International Migration from India*. Princeton, NJ: Princeton University Press.

Kapur, Devesh, with Pratap Bhanu Mehta. 2005. *Public Institutions in India: Performance and Design*. Oxford University Press.

Kerwin, Donald M. 2010. "More than IRCA: US Legalization Programs and the Current Policy Debate." Washington, D.C.: Migration Policy Institute.

Kibria, Nazli. 2002. *Becoming Asian American: Second-Generation Chinese and Korean American Identities*. Baltimore, MD: Johns Hopkins University Press.

——. 2006. "South Asian Americans" In *Asian Americans: Contemporary Trends and Issues*, ed. Pyong Gap Min. Beverly Hills, CA: Sage Publications, pp. 206–27.

——. 2011. *Muslims in Motion: Islam and National Identity in the Bangladeshi Diaspora*. New Brunswick, NJ: Rutgers University Press.

Kim, Claire Jean. 1999. "The Racial Triangulation of Asian Americans." *Politics and Society* 27, 1: 105–38.

——. 2000. *Bitter Fruits: The Politics of Black–Korean Conflict in New York City*. New Haven, CT: Yale University Press.

Kim, Dae Young. 1999. "Beyond Co-Ethnic Solidarity: Mexican and Ecuadorean Employment in Korean-Owned Businesses in New York City." *Ethnic and Racial Studies* 22, 3: 581–605.

Kim, Illsoo. 1980. *New Urban Immigrants: The Korean Community in New York*. Princeton, NJ: Princeton University Press.

Kim, Kwang Chung, and Woo Moo Hurh. 1985. "Ethnic Resources Utilization of Korean Immigrant Entrepreneurs in the Chicago Minority Area." *International Migration Review* 19, 1: 82–111.

Kim, Nadia. 2008. *Imperial Citizens: Koreans and Race from Seoul to LA*. Stanford, CA: Stanford University Press.

Kofman, Eleonore. 2000. "The Invisibility of Skilled Female Migrants and Gender Relations in Studies of Skilled Migration in Europe." *International Journal of Population Geography* 6: 45–59.

Kurien, Prema. 2006. "Multiculturalism and 'American' Religion: The Case of Hindu Indian Americans." *Social Forces* 85, 2: 723–41.

Kusow, Abdi M. 2006. "Migration and Racial Formations Among Somali

References

Immigrants in North America." *Journal of Ethnic and Migration Studies* 32, 3: 533–51.

Lan, P. C. "Among Women: Migrant Domestics and Their Taiwanese Employers Across Generations." In *Global Woman: Nannies, Maids, and Sex Workers in the New Economy*, ed. B. Ehrenreich and A. R. Hochschild. New York: Holt Paperbacks, pp. 169–89.

Lee, Erika. 2003. *At America's Gates: Chinese Immigration During the Exclusion Era 1882–1943*. Chapel Hill: University of North Carolina Press.

Lee, Jennifer. 2002. "From Civil Relations to Racial Conflict: Merchant-Customer Interactions in Urban America," *American Sociological Review* 67: 77–98.

——. 2002. *Civility in the City: Blacks, Jews, and Koreans in Urban America*. Cambridge, MA: Harvard University Press.

Lee, Jennifer, and Frank D. Bean. 2007. "Reinventing the Color Line: Immigration and America's New Racial/Ethnic Divide." *Social Forces* 86: 561–86.

Levitt, Peggy. 2001. *The Transnational Villagers*. Berkeley: University of California Press.

Levitt, Peggy, and B. Nadya Jaworsky. 2007. "Transnational Migration Studies: Past Developments and Future Trends." *Annual Review of Sociology* 33: 129–56.

Levitt, Peggy, and Nina Glick Schiller. 2008. "Conceptualizing Simultaneity: A Transnational Social Field Perspective on Society." In *The Transnational Studies Reader: Intersections and Innovations*, ed. Sanjeev Khagram and Peggy Levitt. New York and London: Routledge, pp. 284–99.

Lichter, Daniel T., and Kenneth Johnson. 2006. "Emerging Rural Settlement Patterns and the Geographic Redistribution of America's New Immigrants." *Rural Sociology* 70: 109–31.

Light, Ivan H. 1984. "Immigrant and Ethnic Enterprise in North America." *Ethnic and Racial Studies* 7: 195–216.

——. 2007. "Global Entrepreneurship and Transnationalism." In *Handbook of Research on Ethnic Minority Entrepreneurship*, ed. Leo-Paul Dana. Cheltenham, UK: Edward Elgar, pp. 3–15

Light, Ivan H., and Edna Bonacich. 1988. *Immigrant Entrepreneurs: Koreans in Los Angeles 1965–1982*. Berkeley: University of California Press.

Light, Ivan H., and Steven J. Gold. 2000. *Ethnic Economies*. Bingley, UK: Emerald Group Publishing.

López, Ann Aurelia. 2007. *The Farmworkers' Journey*. Berkeley and Los Angeles: University of California Press.

Louie, Vivian. 2012. *Keeping the Immigrant Bargain: The Costs and Rewards of Success in America*. New York: The Russell Sage Foundation.

Luthra, Renee R. 2009. "Temporary Immigrants in a High-Skilled Labour Market: A Study of H-1Bs." *Journal of Ethnic and Migration Studies* 35, 2: 227–50.

References

Maldonado, Marta María. 2006. "Racial Triangulation of Latino/a Workers by Agricultural Employers." *Human Organization* 65: 353–61.

——. 2009. "'It Is Their Nature to Do Menial Labour': The Racialization of 'Latino/a Workers' by Agricultural Employers." In *Ethnic and Racial Studies* 32, 6: 1017–36.

Marrow, Helen B. 2009 "New Immigrant Destinations and the American Colour Line." *Ethnic and Racial Studies* 32, 6: 1037–57.

Martin, Philip L. 1994. "Good Intentions Gone Awry: IRCA and U.S. Agriculture." *Annals of the American Academy of Political and Social Science* 534: 44–57.

——. 2002. "Mexican Workers and U.S. Agriculture: The Revolving Door." *International Migration Review* 36: 1124–42.

Massey, Douglas. 1999. "Why Does Immigration Occur? A Theoretical Synthesis." In *Handbook of International Migration: The American Experience*. New York: Russell Sage Foundation.

Massey, Douglas, and Katherine Bartley. 2005. "The Changing Legal Status Distribution of Immigrants: A Caution." *International Migration Review* 39: 469–84.

Massey, Douglas, and Magaly Sanchez. 2010. *Brokered Boundaries: Creating Immigrant Identity in Anti-Immigrant Times*. New York: Russell Sage Foundation.

McCabe, Kristen. 2011. "African Immigrants in the United States." Washington, D.C.: *Migration Policy Institute*. http://www.migrationinformation.org/feature/display.cfm?ID=847#

Menjívar, Cecilia. 2006. "Liminal Legality: Salvadoran and Guatemalan Immigrants' Lives in the United States." *American Journal of Sociology* 111, 4: 999–1037.

Miles, Robert, and Malcolm Brown. 2003 [1989]. *Racism*. New York: Routledge.

Milkman, Ruth. 2011. "Immigrant Workers and the Future of American Labor." *The Labor Lawyer* 26, 2: 295.

Milkman, Ruth, and Kent Wong. 2000. "Organizing the Wicked City: the 1992 Southern California Drywall Strike." In *Organizing Immigrants: The Challenge for Unions in Contemporary California*, ed. Ruth Milkman. Ithaca, NY: Cornell University Press, pp. 169–98.

Min, Pyong Gap. 1984. "From White-Collar Occupations to Small Business: Korean Immigrants' Occupational Adjustment." *Sociological Quarterly* 25: 333–52.

——. 1988. *Ethnic Business Enterprises: Korean Small Business in Atlanta*. New York: Center for Migration Studies.

——. 1992. "The Structure of Social Functions of Korean Immigrant Churches in the United States." *International Migration Review* 26: 1370–94.

——. 1995. "Korean Americans." In *Asian Americans: Contemporary Trends and Issues*, edited by Pyong Gap Min, 199–231. Newbury Park, CA: Sage Publications.

——. 2007. "Korean-Latino Relations in Los Angeles and New York" in *Du Bois Review: Social Science and Research on Race* 4, 2: 395–411.

Mize, Ronald L., and Grace Peña Delgado. 2012. *Latino Immigrants in the United States*. Cambridge, UK: Polity Press.

Model, Suzanne. 1991. "Caribbean Immigrants: A Black Success Story?" *International Migration Review* 25, 2: 248–76.

Moisa, Jennifer. 2008. "Legislative Update: The California DREAM Act and the American DREAM Act." *Children's Legal Rights Journal* 28, 3: 91–3.

Mongar, Randall, and Macreadie Barr. 2009. "Annual Flow Report: Nonimmigrant Admissions to the United States 2008." U.S. Department of Homeland Security, Office of Immigration Statistics. Retrieved June 15, 2009, http://www.dhs.gov/ximgtn/statistics/publications/yearbook.shtm

Moras, Amanda. 2010. "Colour-blind discourses in paid domestic work: foreignness and the delineation of alternative racial markers." *Ethnic and Racial Studies* 33, 2: 233–52.

Motel, Seth, and Eileen Patten. 2012. "The 10 Largest Hispanic Origin Groups: Characteristics, Rankings, Top Counties." Pew Research Hispanic Center: http://www.pewhispanic.org/2012/06/27/the-10-largest-hispanic-orig in-groups-characteristics-rankings-top-counties/

Nagel, Joane. 1994. "Constructing Ethnicity: Creating and Recreating Ethnic Identity and Culture." *Social Problems* 41, 1: 152–76.

Nevins, Joseph. 2002. *Operation Gatekeeper: The Rise of the "Illegal Alien" and the Making of the U.S.-Mexico Boundary*. New York: Routledge.

Ngai, Mae. 2004. *Impossible Subjects: Illegal Aliens and the Making of Modern America*. Princeton, NJ: Princeton University Press.

Nopper, Tamara. 2010. "Colorblind Racism and Institutional Actors' Explanations of Korean Immigrant Entrepreneurship." *Critical Sociology* 36: 65–85. doi:10.1177/0896920509347141

O'Brien, Eileen. 2008. *The Racial Middle: Latinos and Asian Americans Living Beyond the Racial Divide*. New York: New York University Press.

Oh, Joong-Hwan. 2007. "Economic Incentive, Embeddedness and Social Support: A Study of Korean-Owned Nail Salon Workers' Rotating Credit Associations." *International Migration Review* 41: 623–55.

Okihiro, Gary Y. 1994. *Margins and Mainstreams: Asians in American History and Culture*. Seattle: University of Washington Press.

Omi, Michael, and Howard Winant. 1994 [1986]. *Racial Formation in the United States from the 1960s to the 1990s*. New York: Routledge.

Osirim, Mary Johnson. 2012. "African Women in the New Diaspora: Transnationalism and the (Re)Creation of Home." In *Africans in Global Migration: Searching for Promised Lands*, ed. J. A. Arthur, J. Takougang, and T. Owusu. Lanham, MD: Lexington Books, pp. 225–52.

References

Pantoja, Adrian D., Cecilia Menjívar, and Lisa Magaña, 2009. "The Spring Marches of 2006: Latinos, Immigration, and Political Mobilization in the 21st Century." *American Behavioral Scientist* 52, 4.

Park, Lisa S. 2011. *Entitled to Nothing: The Struggle for Immigrant Healthcare in the Age of Welfare Reform.* New York: New York University Press.

Park, Robert E., and Ernest W. Burgess. 1969 [1921]. *Introduction to the Science of Sociology.* Chicago, IL: University of Chicago Press.

Parreñas, Rhacel Salazar. 2005. *Children of Global Migration: Transnational Families and Gendered Woes.* Stanford, CA: Stanford University Press.

Passel, Jeffrey, D'Vera Cohn, and Ana Gonzalez-Barrera. 2012. "Net Migration from Mexico Falls to Zero—and Perhaps Less." Washington, D.C.: Pew Hispanic Center, April.

Pattillo-McCoy, Mary. 1999. *Black Picket Fences: Privilege and Peril among the Black Middle Class.* Chicago, IL: University of Chicago Press.

Peek, Lori. 2005. "Becoming Muslim: The Development of a Religious Identity." *Sociology of Religion* 66, 3: 215–42.

PEW Research Center. 2007. "Muslim Americans: Middle-Class and Mostly Mainstream." Washington, D.C.: PEW Research Center. Retrieved June 8, 2010. http://pewresearch.org/pubs/483/muslim-americans

PEW Research Center. 2012.The Rise of Asian Americans. Washington, D.C.: PEW Research Center. Retrieved March 17, 2013. http://www.pewsocialtrends. org/2012/06/19/the-rise-of-asian-americans/http://www.pewsocialtrends.org/ 2011/07/26/wealth-gaps-rise-to-record-highs-between-whites-blacks-hispanics/

Pieterse, Jan Nederveen. 1998. *White on Black: Images of Africa and Blacks in Western Popular Culture.* New Haven: Yale University Press.

Poros, Maritsa V. 2011. *Modern Migrations: Gujarati Indian Networks in New York and London.* Stanford, CA: Stanford University Press.

Portes, Alejandro, and Robert L. Bach. 1985. *Latin Journey: Cuban and Mexican immigrants in the United States.* Berkeley, CA: University of California Press.

Portes, Alejandro, and Alex Stepick. 1993. *City on the Edge: The Social Transformation of Miami.* Berkeley: University of California Press.

Portes, Alejandro, and R. G. Rumbaut. 2001. *Legacies: The Story of the Immigrant Second Generation.* Berkeley: University of California Press; New York: Russell Sage Foundation.

——. 2006 [1996]. *Immigrant America: A Portrait, 3rd Edition: Revised, Expanded and Updated.* Berkeley: University of California Press.

Portes, Alejandro, and Min Zhou. 1993. "The New Second Generation: Segmented Assimilation and Its Variants Among Post-1965 Immigrant Youth." *The Annals of the American Academy of Political and Social Sciences* 530: 74–96.

Powell, Colin. 2005. "The America I Believe In." National Public Radio. April 11: http://www.npr.org/templates/story/story.php?storyId=4583249

Purkayastha, Bandana. 2005. *Negotiating Ethnicity: Second-Generation South*

References

Asian Americans Traverse a Transnational World. New Brunswick, NJ: Rutgers University Press.

Raijman, Rebeca. 2001. "Mexican Immigrants and Informal Self-Employment in Chicago." *Human Organization* 60: 47–55.

Ramirez, Hernan, and Pierrette Hondagneu-Sotelo. 2009. "Mexican Immigrant Gardeners: Entrepreneurs or Exploited Workers?" *Social Problems* 56: 70–88.

Rangaswamy, Padma. 2007. "South Asians in Dunkin' Donuts: Niche Development in the Franchise Industry." *Journal of Ethnic and Migration Studies* 33, 4: 671–86.

Read, Jen'nan Ghazal. 2008. "The Effects of Post-9/11 Discrimination on Arab-American Racial Identity." In *From Invisibility to Visibility: The Racialization of Arab Americans Before and After September 11th*, ed. N. Naber and A. Jamal. New York: Syracuse University Press.

Rodriguez, Nestor. 2004. "'Workers Wanted': Employer Recruitment of Immigrant Labor." *Work and Occupations* 31: 453–73. doi:10.1177/0730888 404268870.

Roediger, David R. 2007 [1991]. *The Wages of Whiteness: Race and the Making of the American Working Class.* New York: Verso.

Rogers, Reuel. 2001. "'Black Like Who?' Afro-Caribbean Immigrants, African Americans, and the Politics of Group Identity." In *Islands in the City: West Indian Migration to New York*, ed. N. Foner. Berkeley: University of California Press, pp. 163–92.

Romero, Mary. 1992. *Maid in the USA.* New York and London: Routledge, Chapman and Hall.

———. 2008. "'Go After the Women': Mothers Against Illegal Aliens' Campaign Against Mexican Immigrant Women and Their Children." *Indiana Law Journal* 83, 4. Available at: http://www.repository.law.indiana.edu/ilj/vol83/iss4/8.

Rosenblum, Marc, and Lang Hoyt. 2011. "The Basics of E-Verify, the US Employer Verification System." *Migration Policy Institute: Migration Information Source.* Retrieved April 4, 2013. http://www.migrationinformation.org/featu re/display.cfm?ID=846

Roth, Wendy D. 2012. *Race Migrations: Latinos and the Cultural Transformation of Race.* Stanford, CA: Stanford University Press.

Said, Edward. 1978. *Orientalism.* New York: Pantheon Books.

Sanchez, George J. 1999. "Race, Nation, and Culture in Recent Immigration Studies." *Journal of American Ethnic History* 18(4): 66–84.

Saxenian, AnnaLee. 1999 "Beyond Boundaries: Open Labor Markets and Learning in Silicon Valley." In *Boundaryless Careers: Work, Mobility, and Learning in the New Organizational Era*, ed. M. Arthur and D. Rousseau. New York: Oxford University Press.

———. 2002. "Silicon Valley's New Immigrant High-Grown Entrepreneurs." *Economic Development Quarterly* 16, 1: 20–31.

———. 2006. *The New Argonauts: Regional Advantage in a Global Economy.* Cambridge, MA: Harvard University Press.

Schrag, Peter. 2010. *Not Fit for Our Society: Nativism and Immigration.* Berkeley: University of California Press.

Schrieke, B. 1936. *Alien Americans: A Study of Race Relations.* New York: The Viking Press.

Shaw-Taylor, Yoku. 2007. "The Intersection of Assimilation, Race, Presentation of Self, and Transnationalism in America." In *The Other African Americans: Contemporary African and Caribbean Immigrants in the United States*, ed., Y. Shaw-Taylor and S. A. Tuch. Lanham, MD: Rowman & Littlefield, pp. 1–47

Shih, Johanna. 2007. "Job-Hopping: Social Networks in the Global High-Tech Industry." In *Constructing Borders/Crossing Boundaries: Race, Ethnicity and Immigration*, ed. C. Brettel. Lanham, MD: Lexington Books, pp. 219–41.

Sivanandan, Ambalavener. 1989. "Racism 1992." *Race & Class* 30, 3: 85–90.

Sklair, Leslie. 2001. *The Transnational Capitalist Class.* Oxford: Blackwell.

Smedley, Audrey. 2007. *Race in North America: Origin and Evolution of a Worldview.* Boulder, CO: Westview Press.

Smith, Lamar. 2012. *Fact Sheet: The STEM Jobs Act (H.R. 6429).* United States House of Representatives Judiciary Committee. Retrieved March 4, 2013. http://judiciary.house.gov/issues/STEM/112012%20Fact%20Sheet%20 on%20STEM%20Bill.pdf

Smith, Robert Courtney. 2006. *Mexican New York: Transnational Lives of New Immigrants.* Berkeley: University of California Press.

Song, Miri. 2004. "Introduction: Who's At the Bottom? Examining Claims About Racial Hierarchy." *Ethnic and Racial Studies* 27: 859–77.

Stepick, Alex. 1989."Shading Objective Reality: Public Presentation on Haitian Boat People." *Human Organization* 48, 1: 91–4.

Stepick, Alex, Carol D. Stepick, Emmanuel Eugene, Deborah Teed, and Yves Labissiere. 2001. "Shifting Identities." In *Ethnicities: Children of Immigrants in Immigrant America*, ed. Rubén Rumbaut and Alejandro Portes. Berkeley: University of California Press; and New York: Russell Sage Foundation, pp. 229–66

Summers Sandoval, T. F. 2008. "Disobedient Bodies: Racialization, Resistance, and the Mass (Re)Articulation of the Mexican Immigrant Body." *American Behavioral Scientist* 52, 4.

Takaki, Ronald T. 1998. *Strangers from a Different Shore: A History of Asian Americans.* Boston: Little, Brown.

Taras, Raymond. 2013. " 'Islamophobia never stands still': Race, Religion and Culture." *Ethnic and Racial Studies* 36, 3: 417–34.

Telles, Edward E., and Vilma Ortiz. 2008. *Generations of Exclusion: Mexican Americans, Assimilation, and Race.* New York: Russell Sage Foundation.

References

Thai, Hung Cam. 2008. *For Better or for Worse: Vietnamese International Marriages in the New Global Economy*. Rutgers, NJ, and London: Rutgers University Press.

Thomas, Kevin J. A. 2012. *A Demographic Profile of Black Caribbean Immigrants in the United States*. Washington, D.C.: Migration Policy Institute.

Tilly, Charles. 1998. *Durable Inequality*. Berkeley: University of California Press.

Tuan, Mia. 1998. *Forever Foreigners or Honorary Whites? The Asian Ethnic Experience Today*. New Brunswick, NJ: Rutgers University Press.

Tyner, James A. 1999. "The Global Context of Gendered Labor Migration from the Philippines to the United States." *American Behavioral Scientist* 42, 4: 671–89.

Urban, Andrew. 2009. "Irish Domestic Servants, 'Biddy' and Rebellion in the American Home, 1850–1900." *Gender and History* 21, 2: 263–86.

Urban League. 2009. http://www.cnn.com/2009/US/03/25/black.america.report/

Usdansky, Margaret L., and Thomas J. Espenshade. 2001. "The Evolution of U.S. Policy Toward Employment-Based Immigrants and Temporary Workers: The H-1B Debate in Historical Perspective." In *The International Migration of the Highly Skilled: Demand, Supply, and Development Consequences in Sending and Receiving Countries*, ed. W. A. Cornelius, T. J. Espenshade, and I. Salehyan. La Jolla, CA: Centre for Comparative Immigration Studies, University of California, San Diego.

U.S. Department of Homeland Security. 2008. *Yearbook of Immigration Statistics: 2007*. Washington, D.C.: U.S. Department of Homeland Security, Office of Immigration.

U.S. Department of Homeland Security. 2011. *Yearbook of Immigration Statistics: 2010*. Washington, D.C.: U.S. Department of Homeland Security, Office of Immigration.

Valdez, Zulema. 2011. *The New Entrepreneurs: How Race, Class, and Gender Shape American Enterprise*. Stanford, CA: Stanford University Press.

Varma, Roli. 2011. "Transnational Migration and Entrepreneurialism: Indians in the U.S. Technology Sector." *Perspectives on Global Development and Technology* 10, 2: 270–87.

Vickerman, Milton. 1999. *Crosscurrents: West Indian Immigrants and Race*. Oxford: Oxford University Press.

Wadhwa, Vivek, Guillermina Jasso, Ben Rissing, Gary Gereffi, and Richard Freeman. 2007. "Intellectual Property, the Immigration Backlog, and a Reverse Brain-Drain: America's New Immigrant Entrepreneurs, Part III." Available at SSRN: http://ssrn.com/abstract=1008366

Waldinger, Roger David. 1999. *Still the Promised City?* Cambridge, MA: Harvard University Press.

Waldinger, Roger, and Michael Lichter. 2003. *How the Other Half Works:*

References

Immigration and the Social Organization of Labor. Berkeley: University of California Press.

Warren, Jonathan W., and France Winddance Twine. 1997. "White Americans, the New Minority?: Non-Blacks and the Ever-Expanding Boundaries of Whiteness." *Journal of Black Studies* 28: 200–18.

Waters, Mary C. 1990. *Ethnic Options: Choosing Identities in America.* Berkeley, CA: University of California Press.

——. 1996. "Optional Ethnicities: For Whites Only?" In *Ethnicity in America,* ed. Silvia Pedraza and Ruben Rumbaut. Belmont, CA: Wadsworth, pp. 444–54.

——. 1999. *Black Identities: West Indian Immigrant Dreams and American Realities.* Cambridge, MA: Harvard University Press.

Weiner, Melissa F. 2012. "Towards a Critical Global Race Theory." *Sociology Compass* 6, 4: 332–50.

West, Cornel. 1995. Foreword to *Critical Race Theory: The Key Writings That Formed the Movement,* ed. Crenshaw, Gotanda, Peller, Thomas. New York: The New Press.

Williams, Raymond B. 1988. *Religions of Immigrants from India and Pakistan: New Threads in the American Tapestry.* New York: Cambridge University Press.

Wimmer, Andreas, and Nina Glick Schiller. "Methodological Nationalism, the Social Sciences, and the Study of Migration: An Essay in Historical Epistemology. In *The Transnational Studies Reader: Intersections and Innovations,* ed. Sanjeev Khagram and Peggy Levitt. New York and London: Routledge, pp. 104–17.

Winant, Howard. 2000. "Race and Race Theory." *Annual Review of Sociology* 26: 169–85.

——. 2001. *The World as a Ghetto: Race and Democracy since World War II.* New York: Basic Books.

Wolgin, Philip E. 2011. "Seen and (Mostly) Unseen: The True Costs of E-Verify." *Center for American Progress.* Retrieved April 4, 2013. http://www.americanprogress.org/issues/immigration/report/2011/06/27/9858/seen-and-mostly-unseen/.

Yoon, In-Jin. 1997. *On My Own: Korean Businesses and Race Relations in America.* Chicago: University of Chicago Press.

Zamudio, Margaret M., and Michael I. Lichter. 2008. "Bad Attitudes and Good Soldiers: Soft Skills as a Code for Tractability in the Hiring of Immigrant Latina/os over Native Blacks in the Hotel Industry." *Social Problems* 55: 573–89.

Zenner, Walter. 1991. *Minorities in the Middle: A Cross-Cultural Analysis.* Albany, NY: State University of New York Press.

Zlolniski, Christian. 2003. "Labor Control and Resistance of Mexican Immigrant Janitors in Silicon Valley." *Human Organization* 62, 1: 39–49.

References

Zolberg, Aristide R. 2007. "Immigration Control Policy: Law and Implementation." In *The New Americans: A Guide to Immigration since 1965*, ed. Mary C. Waters, Reed Ueda, and Helen B. Marrow. Cambridge, MA: Harvard University Press.

Index

191

Index

Index

Index